SELECTED POEMS

GOETHE

————————

SELECTED POEMS

Translated by
JOHN WHALEY

Introduced by
MATTHEW BELL
King's College, University of London

J. M. Dent   London

First published in Great Britain in 1998
by J. M. Dent

Translation © 1998 John Whaley
Introduction and other critical apparatus © 1998 Matthew Bell
The moral right of John Whaley and Matthew Bell to be identified
as the authors of this work has been asserted in accordance with
the Copyright, Designs and Patents Act of 1988

A CIP catalogue record for this book
is available from the British Library.

ISBN 0 460 87917 0

Consultant editor for this volume
T. J. Reed
Queen's College, Oxford

Typeset by Deltatype Limited, Birkenhead, Merseyside
Set in Sabon
Printed and bound in Great Britain by
Butler & Tanner Ltd, Frome and London

J. M. Dent

Weidenfeld & Nicolson
The Orion Publishing Group Ltd
Orion House
5 Upper Saint Martin's Lane
London WC2H 9EA

CONTENTS

INTRODUCTION

Goethe was born in Frankfurt-am-Main on 28 August 1749 and died in Weimar at the age of 82, having outlived almost all of his contemporaries. The world from which he passed in 1832 was very different from the world into which he had been born. Europe in the middle of the eighteenth century had been a picture of stability. Louis XV sat splendid and secure on the French throne. Under the Austrian Habsburgs, the Holy Roman Empire of the German Nation provided a kind of ramshackle cohesion for the German-speaking territories. The greatest shock for the mid-eighteenth-century mind, the Lisbon earthquake of 1755, was a natural, not a political disaster. But all sense of a politically stable world was destroyed by the French Revolution. The Revolution created the modern politics of left and right and encouraged the liberatory impulses of atheism, feminism, and the questioning of institutions such as marriage. The Holy Roman Empire formally ceased to exist in 1806, along with all but one of the ancient German bishoprics and archbishoprics and the right of about 350 Imperial Knights to appeal directly to the Emperor. Towards the end of Goethe's life, the new ideologies of socialism, communism, and anarchism were formulated. But Goethe was born five years after the death of Alexander Pope; he was eighteen when Voltaire died; Samuel Johnson died six years later. During Goethe's lifetime that culture of polish and wit – no matter that it only ever half-concealed the chaos beneath – was destroyed by Romanticism. In music, a similar development led from the Bach family, headed by Johann Sebastian (d. 1750), to Mozart (1756–91), Beethoven (1770–1827), Schubert (1797–1828), and Schumann (1810–56). The leading lights of Enlightenment science were Newton and Linnaeus. In the mid-eighteenth century, nature, like politics, seemed orderly and static. But by the time of Goethe's death chemistry and biology, the sciences of transformation, were established. The *Beagle* was heading south down the coast of Brazil when Goethe died.

Goethe was directly and continuously involved with these changes. Often he was not on the winning side, and sometimes he quite misjudged the direction of change. But his interest in the changes that took place during his lifetime was omnivorous. Less directly, his poems mirrored and fed back into that process, via his influence on Romantic writing and music (though he did not count himself a Romantic) and on his readers at large. In the course of his eighty-two years he wrote thousands of poems. As a poet he was as industrious as his age. More impressive than the quantity of his poems, though, is the variety of their forms, subjects, and moods. Goethe's poetry has many different voices and no obvious single distinguishing mark. In this he stands apart from contemporaries of equal rank such as Hölderlin, Keats, or Shelley. These are poets for whom authenticity means purity of voice; unsightly reminders of the mundane and the modern are tidied away. The result of the Romantic quest for authenticity was that around 1800 the untidy stuff of modern life started to migrate from poetry to the novel. Here Goethe's resistance to the trend was salutary. Much of his poetry has a simple verbal surface with which ordinary and modern things create no dissonance. The quality of these poems is discrete: it may be a rhythm that makes ordinary speech break into dance, or a sudden, unexpected realisation that there is depth behind naivety. Where more elaborate effects are used – the most common is a strangely Romantic form of classicism – the modern world can still be included without discord. The poem 'Winter Journey in the Harz', which strikingly revives classical metaphor and mood, carries a reference to eighteenth-century road-building without losing its footing. In 'The Diary', a deceptively light comic narrative, to convey the grace of the young woman who unwittingly tempts the diarist, Goethe describes her carving a chicken.

When we try to map this long poetic career, it is tempting to lose ourselves in the wealth of detail surrounding Goethe's life, our knowledge of which exceeds even the biographer's wildest dreams; but this wealth can turn out to be a mixed blessing. We know that before Goethe climbed the Brocken in December 1777, he visited and sought to help a melancholic young philosopher F. V. L. Plessing, who stands behind the character 'first despised, and now too a despiser' in 'Winter Journey in the Harz'. In the nineteenth century it was customary for the poems to be served up with all sorts of biographical appetisers of this kind. At its best this makes the poetry as flat as biography. It tempts us to commit the 'genetic fallacy' of valuing the poems in terms of their origins rather than their actual qualities. At its worst it is as intrusive and hypocritical as biography can be. It asks the reader to sit in judgement over the life, at the same time as vicariously experiencing the life through the poems. What, then, should we make of the relationship between Goethe's life and his poems? In his autobiography Goethe calls the poems 'fragments of a great confession'. The autobiography was intended to explain the actions that made these poetic confessions necessary. In answer to this the careful critic might say that autobiography and poetry should be read differently: we read the poems for what they are, not for any autobiographical details that lie behind them. Goethe took the more fragile and creative view that autobiography was somehow continuous with poetry. He called his autobiography – at least that portion of it which reached from his birth to his move to Weimar in 1775 – *Poetry and Truth*. Goethe said of the autobiography to his friend Eckermann in 1831: 'These are the results of my life pure and simple, and the facts that are recounted only serve to confirm a higher truth ... I thought there were some symbols of human life in there. I called the book *Poetry and Truth* because a higher tendency lifts it out of the realm of base reality ... A fact about our life is valid not insofar as it is true but insofar as it signifies something.' If that sounds portentous, it has more to do with Goethe the man than Goethe the poet: all good autobiography has to make the data of a life into something more general. In the same way, but in a manner peculiar to its own form, each poem is distilled from life into a symbolic life-story. Goethe drew on his own life because that happened to be the most immediate and authentic material for a meditation on the shape of human life in general. That in turn is important because reality – the building of a good road, the carving of a chicken – is the ballast that stops a poem floating airily off into abstraction. An attitude of good faith towards the texture of reality can earn a poet the right to sing a more ambitious song. In his poems Goethe speaks from experience of the world that he, as a particular individual, inhabits, and he makes that experience complex, reflective, and representative.

At the heart of Goethe's poetry is the philosophical and scientific concern of the eighteenth century (and since) with explaining how the complexity of human life might be patterned. This work of reconciling complexity and a simple organising principle is the theme of the 1817 poem 'Primal Words, Orphic'. Convention and our ingrained binary habits of thought divide the forces that determine human life into two classes: love and strife, necessity and free-will, nature and nurture. Goethe has five 'primal' categories: Fate, Chance, Love, Necessity, and Hope. These are described in separate stanzas, each with its own lapidary Greek heading. There is grandeur in this poem's manner, but not grandiosity. The high tone of some of Goethe's poetry – and not just of the later work:

it is already there in 'Ganymede' (1774) and 'The Divine' (1783) – is neither unearned nor superior. The verbal texture of 'Primal Words, Orphic' is marked by the labour of taking in the world's complexity. As well as identifying categories for our experience of life, the five stanzas follow a life-story: birth, growing up, the entry into adulthood, adulthood itself, and old age. Two principles of organisation, the logical and the narrative, are thus laid over one another. This combining of logical and narrative arguments creates a complex whole, and it is repeated at the verbal level, where pairs of simple concepts (the self and the 'law' of fate, 'time' and 'power') are fashioned into one complex concept, 'imprinted form informing living matter', which holds them in intertwined suspension. The dynamic nature of chance is expressed by the replacement of nouns by verbs (*Wandelndes* by *wandelt*, *Tand* by *durchgetandelt*), as if the fixed structure of grammar were changing, and the fourth stanza, on Necessity, plays with words of related meaning and appearance (*wollten*, *Wille*, *Wollen*, *sollten*, *Willkür*, *Muß*, and so on) to suggest a language both confined in fixed forms and free to change and combine.

This kind of conspicuous verbal richness is rare. Here and in a small number of other poems – 'Why give us deep vision … ?', 'Nature and Art', 'Schiller's Remains' – the architectural feel of the language is the signal that we are in the boundary area between what science and sense can tell us and what we can only intuit. What these poems share with the main body of Goethe's work is that they dwell on boundaries. More typically these are boundaries between emotional or psychological territories. It was from this that the first generation of Romantics in England and Germany developed a poetics of spiritual crisis around 1800. From the perspective of Romanticism, the moderate temper of Goethe's classicism might seem tame. But boundaries are not necessarily extremes. It is important to recognise that Goethe's avoidance of extreme inwardness derived from his fascination with the boundaries between self and other, between duty and love, reality and imagination, our responsibilities to society and 'the pleasure …/That by other men not known/Or not judged aright,/Roams the labyrinthine zone/Of the heart at night' ('To the Moon').

'The Diary' (1810) shows Goethe's versatility in handling moments of crisis in human development. The poem is, in the first place, a well-paced comic narrative in the manner of the later eighteenth century, headed by a Latin tag and laced with what then counted as obscenity. Away from his wife, the diarist feels tempted into infidelity by a young woman, but he cannot perform. She dozes off, and he recalls the early days of his love for his wife, including his scandalous erection before the altar on his wedding his wife, including his scandalous erection before the altar on his wedding day. Now he is aroused, but he stops short of waking the woman because he realises that he owes his arousal to the memories of his wife. The poem closes with the routinely drawn moral that love is a stronger force than duty. But beneath its lascivious and mock-philosophical surface, this is a serious poem about morality, or at least about what morality is not. The poem opens with the phlegmatic observation that we may all be sinners. But this is promptly countered with the view that timely redemption comes in the vague form of 'some power' that makes us all virtuous. The diarist is saved from actual adultery by the power – or the lack of it – that is his sexuality. But this opens up the possibility that the poem's morality, far from being clear, shares the rich ambiguity that is so characteristic of Goethe's writing. The closer we look, the less clear it is what the 'duty' and the 'love' in the poem's moral refer to. Is duty the moral debt the diarist owes to his wife and love the physical force that keeps him (albeit only technically) true to her? Or is it love for the young woman that arouses him and makes him want to satisfy her, before the voice of duty calls? Or is it his duty to satisfy the woman, who clearly expects as much? Or does love (or its ingredient lust) attract him to the girl and overcome his duty to his wife? Whatever one makes of this indeterminacy, it clearly both wrecks the duty-based morality that brands us all sinners and weakens the diarist's own naturalistic morality that would make us all saints. Even the truthfulness of the diary referred to in the title is questioned. Instead of reporting the night's events, as by rights it ought, the diary offers the diarist's wife a single line: 'Only by sickness is health validated'. True, and clever, as far as it goes, but much less honest and interesting than the poem that bears its name and of which it is a part. For the poem does much more than the neo-classical tale of 'virtue preserved' that it resembles. It is fair to see in the poem's complexity a scepticism about received wisdom and conventional patterns of thought. The rejection of 'routine thinking' was what impressed Matthew Arnold about Goethe.[1] For Goethe, routine thinking stands between us and an intenser experience of life. Many of the poems are experiments in disencumbering the self of all that is merely routine. It was this side of Goethe that also appealed to Nietzsche.

Goethe's path away from routine leads in two directions: towards the more meditative voice of 'Primal Words, Orphic', and towards a simpler, more immediate poetry. Like 'Primal Words, Orphic', 'The Diary' implies a view of the poetic imagination as more truthful than prosaic common sense. These poems nod in the direction of Romanticism and its tendency to lionise the poet's imagination, and were this typical of Goethe, it would support the Anglo-Saxon habit of treating him as a Romantic. But

Romantic views. There is a tangibility and approachability about most of Goethe's poetry that is thoroughly unlike Romanticism. The imagination is not a launch-pad for otherworldly adventures. There is nothing in Goethe's poetic work even remotely like Coleridge's 'Kubla Khan'. In its positive aspect the imagination is a tool for extracting a maximum of richness from the world. In its negative aspect, an aspect that is foreign to Romanticism, it is a poison that chokes off the life-blood of experience. 'The New Amadis' (1774) is one of a number of poems that present the imagination's poisonous aspect. The poem's 'I' is a modern counterpart of the adventuring Amadis of sixteenth-century Iberian romance, and he escapes from the confinement of childhood into a boy's imaginary world peopled with characters out of French fairy tales, a world that is bound to collapse because this 'new' Amadis belongs to the illusion-puncturing age of Enlightenment. But the collapse of his fantasy is not accompanied by rationalistic gloating. The tone is realistic and sympathetic. Amadis's imaginary world mixes playfulness with a measure of masculine destruc-tiveness and, for all its liberatory potential, a new form of imprisonment, this time within his imagination:

> And her kiss was Heaven's bread,
> Glowing like the wine,
> Oh! I loved till nearly dead
> Whilst round her the sun did shine
> Painted in gold leaf.

> Oh, who took her, who the thief?
> Could no magic band
> Her false flight gainsay?
> Tell me, where now is her land,
> How to find the way?

This is how the poem ends, hanging in the emptiness of loss. It leaves us with a sight of how painful growing up and of how unstable imaginings of maleness can be. Goethe conveys the danger of the imagination without breaking the poem's naive surface, as a German Romantic might have felt bound to do. The poem derives its force from Goethe's un-Romantic refusal to undermine Amadis's voice. The voice remains plausible and particular; it is an identity, not a style or the 'objective' perspective of an outsider looking in.

The ability to invent personalities gives to much of Goethe's poetry a theatrical flavour. (Goethe's plays are often criticised for their lyrical character, but it is truer to say that the lyrics are enriched by the influence of drama.) At the core of Goethe's poetry throughout his career is a commentary on the shape of human life in the modern world. But these poems are fascinatiang because the poet comments on life from within life, from the perspective of one who shares the flaws and delusions of his subjects and who, like them, is engaged in the perplexing unfinished business of understanding the world.

*

The earliest surviving picture of Goethe, from 1762, shows him posing with his family in a pastoral scene. The twelve-year-old Wolfgang stands with his sister Cornelia behind the parents and in front of an overgrown classical ruin. Dressed as a shepherd, he is patting a sheep. Of course, this could be any upper middle-class German (or French or British) family, fossilised for posterity in the idyllic style to which they aspired, safely insulated from the busy, dirty city that was their real habitat. Not that this ideal was hopelessly out of step with the life of the Goethe family: in 1755, Johann Caspar Goethe, Wolfgang's father, had the rambling family home – its half-timbered front overhanging the cobbled street and cluttered by ad hoc extensions – updated with a tidy, neo-classical facade. The son of a self-made man and married to the daughter of one of Frankfurt's patricians, Goethe's father had travelled in Italy, and the father's fashionable taste for the classical style was taken on by his son (albeit in a revolutionised form that would have appalled the father). Even so, the portrait of the Goethe family strikes one as a sad and false affair, a small provincial version of the pastoral charade acted out some twenty years later by Louis XVI and Marie-Antoinette at Versailles in pathetic isolation from the now revolutionary world. It belongs to the mid-eighteenth-century culture of sensibility (*Empfindsamkeit* in Germany), which practised a small repertoire of emotions – above all sympathy and a delicate melancholy – and a refined sensitivity to art and 'improved' nature. The natural style of the English country garden is characteristic of the age, with its use of distant prospects and fake ruins to create feelings of loss and longing.

Goethe's tendency towards self-dramatisation was fed from other sources too. He credited to his mother his ability to tell stories, and at the age of five he was given his own puppet theatre. Later, in the novel *Wilhelm Meister's Apprenticeship* and the autobiography *Poetry and Truth*, he dwelt on the theatrical pursuits of his youth. From these flowed the facility in inventing and staging new voices that distinguishes the early poems in particular. The fashion of sensibility, limited though it was to a vocabulary of sighs, tears, and ecstasy, did encourage imaginative empathy. The poet could exercise his feelings in creating a new self with its own stormily changeable emotional life. Admittedly much of the German writing done in this spirit reads like *Tristram Shandy* without the humour and inventiveness. Perhaps the best expression of German *Empfindsamkeit* are the Hamburg symphonies of C. P. E. Bach (1714–88).

Goethe's achievement was to re-invigorate what had degraded to a style. In these earliest poems, the experience of love, still emotionally limited and caught in a cycle of unfulfillable desire and loss, belongs to a particular individual in a dramatically imagined situation, rather than some generic lover trapped in the amber of pastoral idyll. In the poem 'Meeting and Parting' (p. 5), the lover riding through the night to a tryst with his beloved runs the gauntlet of his own inflated imaginings. There is still the tendency in this early poem to 'improve' nature with metaphor, but it is fresh metaphor, a sort of homespun Gothic which softens with a touching naivety the poet's self-dramatisation: the first-time romantic lead galloping unsteadily out of the comforting maternal evening into the frenetically self-assertive night-time of male desire. Even here Goethe can hint at a subterranean story of male awakening. Not that sexuality can ever emerge. By morning our hero is re-integrated into the asexual culture of sensibility which created him. The poem closes with him tearfully looking on as the meeting ends and his beloved departs. He can only offer conventional thanks to the gods of idyll for this mutuality of feeling.

The poems of Goethe's late teens and early twenties have their own immediacy born of naturalness of rhythm and freshness of language. In this immediacy we can also sense joy in an alternative to the legal studies which Goethe pursued unenthusiastically first in Leipzig, then in Strasbourg and at the Imperial courts in Wetzlar, at his father's direction. The potential for something more substantial was realised when Goethe was introduced by the philosopher Johann Gottfried Herder (1744–1803) to the latest linguistic and cultural thinking of the French Enlightenment. Herder's own *Treatise on the Origin of Language* (1772) shared the new fashion for primitivism, the belief (crudely put) that morality can only be rescued if we return to the natural human impulses that civilisation has imprisoned and disciplined in the name of progress. For Herder, language originates in the animal expression of joy, pain, and desire. The bleating of sheep, once mood-music for the pastoral scene, is now an expression of raw ovine emotion and a primitive precursor of our own massively complex and artificial linguistic world. The new theory also had its literary canon: Homer, Pindar, Shakespeare, Ossian – the last ironically an eighteenth-century fake collection of ancient Highland lays designed to appeal to precisely this taste for primitives and 'Original Geniuses'. All of these poetic 'naturals', Herder argued, were able, through their contact with the primitive sources of language, to cut through convention and reach down to the emotional substrate of human existence.

The friendship with Herder gave Goethe cause to exercise his gift for self-dramatisation on a grander scale. In the early 1770s in Strasbourg, Wetzlar and Frankfurt, a series of works, few of which progressed far at first, grew around the figure of the *Alleingänger*, the character who disregards convention to go it alone: Prometheus; Julius Caesar; the wandering Jew, Ahasuerus; Götz von Berlichingen, the feuding knight with the iron hand; the vilified necromancer Faust; Egmont, the fighter for Dutch independence; and Goethe's own invention, the frustrated lover and artist Werther. Werther sentimentally (and wrongly) supposes that the venerated world will reward the artist. Driven by an imaginative empathy that has spun free of its bearings, he is haunted to suicide by the gap between the warm world of feeling and the cold world of reality. *The Sufferings of Young Werther* is commonly mistaken for a sentimental hymn to unrequited love, but in the first place it shows that Goethe was aware of the tragic potential of the *Alleingänger*. Goethe's enthusiasm for Herder's philosophy was matched by his scepticism towards its fundamentalist claims about society and the absurd literal-mindedness of the call 'back to nature'. The satirical playlet *Satyros, or the Idolized Demon of the Woods* (1773, p. 11) presents both faces of the new philosophy. The hermit takes pleasure in his ability to out-endure the werewolves in winter; his is a refreshingly down-to-earth view of rural survival. His counterpart Satyros, prophet of a back-to-nature creed which he expounds in a hugely energetic cosmogony, is revealed as a self-serving zealot. In the figure of Satyros, Goethe exposes his own enthusiasm for Herder's philosophy of beginnings to a sharp critique. Like the self-serving god against whom Prometheus rages (p. 19), Satyros exploits people's willingness to believe for his own gratification. The charisma of the *Alleingänger* is as dangerous as the poisonous conventionality that he disregards. That is by way of a cautionary reminder; the poetic lessons of Herder's theory stuck fast. *Satyros* has all the rawness appropriate to the new poetry: it tells a story of beginnings with rhythmic drive and in colloquial language, complete with the mandatory obscenities. (Götz von Berlichingen shouted down to the soldiers besieging his fortress to kiss his arse). It was with Herder's help that Goethe mastered the difficult art of appearing spontaneous.

Goethe's early poems are concerned above all with the solitary lover trapped in a world shaped by the feeling imagination. These poems – 'The New Amadis', 'New Love, New Life', 'Lili's Park', 'On the Lake' – radiate from the central paradox of the lover's need to escape, not so much from emotional commitment, as from the power of his own imagination to gild the experience and memory of a love that is essentially unfulfilling. The temptation to indulge the imagination, as Werther does, is always present. To prevent spontanteity from lapsing into reverie, to give structure to the feeling imagination, Goethe, even at this early stage, chose classical self-limitation and restraint. The literary models were Homer and Pindar – Goethe never seriously tried to imitate Ossian, whereas in 1772 he writes to Herder of 'living in' Pindar – and the technique which he prized was that of extended metaphor. The natural world becomes a model, which, more than any mere decorative instance, has a force and independence that gives moral direction to human life. Harshly resistant or comfortingly stable, nature is the medium against which the unstable imagination can reform itself. The outside world is an objective; it demands that the human self echo its rhythms. (See 'On the Lake', p. 31.)

By 1775 Goethe was chafing at the legal career which his father hoped would lead him to Frankfurt's top administrative position. An engagement had also gone sadly wrong. Then came the offer of a position as mentor to the young Duke Karl August of Sachsen-Weimar (a small, poor, but strategically located German territory), and with it the opportunity for Goethe to test himself, more ambitiously, against the resistant medium of politics in a petty principality. At first his energies were spent in entertaining and restraining the wayward Duke, but Goethe soon made himself politically indispensable and in 1782 was elevated to the role of President of Chamber and to the nobility. Readers have often felt that the poetry of the early Weimar years inhabits an entirely imagined world. The great elegy 'Why give us deep vision . . . ?' (p. 33) meditates on and arms itself against this free fall of the imagination out of the real world into the half-light of uncertain memory. Support comes not from nature but from some wonderfully balanced rhetoric organised in the service of an argument that veers close to paradox and a mind that is struggling to keep itself whole. But another, altogether different voice emerges alongside this in the period after 1775, and it speaks with a moral authority that is new for Goethe. The tone is religious, the form adapted from Pindar's odes. Wilfully difficult of comprehension, poems such as 'Winter Journey in the Harz' and 'The Divine' (pp. 39 and 45) celebrate a world that is itself difficult and harsh and, for that reason, rewarding. 'Winter Journey in the Harz' might be a set text on the progress of the modern poet. The poet must avoid misanthropic self-obsession and the easy vacuousness of submerging himself in society. The only way is to climb through the harsh, purifying medium of nature to the mountain-top, 'mysterious and evident' ('*geheimnisvoll offenbar*'). Poetry makes a truth that is evident and mysterious, hidden and revealed in its form. As well as their jagged syntax and stark imagery, the poems derive their circular shape from Pindar's odes. They end by returning to their beginning, but on a higher plane, in the form of an ascending spiral, and in this way they give voice to a measured optimism.

Much later Goethe would write a scientific essay on the spiral tendency of plant growth. 'Winter Journey' is also a scientist's poem. Goethe's most important discovery of the first ten years in Weimar was that poetry and science were natural allies. This gave a new aspect to the idea that the imagination must test itself against nature. The scientific character of Goethe's poetry is its movement from self to world and back, like the scientist's continual cross-referring between evidence and theory. After 1775 Goethe began to study geology (hence the stiff climb in 'Winter Journey'), anatomy, and botany. The last of these proved the most rewarding. Goethe stumbled across a formative debate in the infant science of biology between the theories of 'preformation' (organic development is the unfolding of a core essence) and 'epigenesis' (development is the interaction between an organism and its environment). This was similar to the nature-nurture debate in the psychology of education, which Goethe knew well, and close to his own interest in the poetry of human development. The fact that the debates ran parallel confirmed Goethe in his view – proclaimed ecstatically after he identified the intermaxillary bone in the human mouth whose absence in humans, it had previously been argued, separated them from other mammals – that humans were part of a natural continuum. The rarely and hesitantly spoken premise of Goethe's new interest in science was that the natural world is our human horizon and that only nature can point us to the fate of our souls. In this there is a conscious act of self-restraint, but there is also recompense for the loss involved in renouncing theology, for nature does at least provide a stable reference point in the changeable world of human fashions. As Goethe put it in a letter to his friend Knebel, 'the consistency of nature is a fine consolation for the inconsistency of human beings'.[2]

The relevance of that consolation grew during the early 1780s, as the exercise of limited authority in a poor principality clogged by vested interests became intolerable. Goethe spent the middle years of the decade on an extended furlough in Italy, travelling as far south as Sicily and spending a long period educating himself as an artist in Rome. Superficially, the Italian journey appears to repeat his father's travels: the Grand Tour that rounds off a young man's education and secures for him tastes and accomplishments befitting his status at home. But Goethe's stay in

Italy was characteristically unconventional. Like every tourist he ticked off the sights in the guide books, and he learnt how to appreciate classical and neo-classical architecture, but with an enquiring creativity entirely his own. What interested him was how the art of Italy could be broken down into a repertoire of elementary forms and how these were produced by particular geographical and human circumstances. The orders of Greek temple-building corresponded, in a way, to the elementary forms of animal anatomy or plant structure. Morphology – the science that isolates basic forms and relates each to functions determined by the living environment – applied to humans as to plants. There was nothing new then in claiming that human culture was shaped by its material circumstances (nor is there now anything old-fashioned about it). Goethe's insight was that our lives are organised, at a deep level, by the formative events of birth, reproduction, and death. Human life, with all of its inconsistencies, really could be grasped as a part of nature, if we could only acknowledge the power of our natural selves in shaping our behaviour.

Goethe believed that this way of thinking favoured classicism as an artistic project: he read classical authors, in particular the Latin poets, in their natural habitat, and the freedom with which they spoke about the human body made him aware of how deadening modern moral sensibilities could be. They confirmed to him that there were universals in human life which the study of individual cultures would reveal, and that closest to these was a style of artistic creation which put form on a par with content, balanced the predictability of a fixed convention against the surprise of innovation, and exercised restraint on the imagination by setting the human spirit against the analogue of nature. The Italian journey began the period of Goethe's 'high' classicism. He practised the use of classical metres, especially the elegiac couplet with its even tread and long breath, the longer hexameter line rising to a strong climax, and the pentameter falling gently to a resolution. And he produced, in the *Roman Elegies* and the *Venetian Epigrams*, two of the most extraordinary lyric cycles in modern poetry. The two cycles are in some ways mirror images. The *Elegies* (named thus for their form, rather than their content) tell how the poet's casual sexual liaison with a young Roman woman develops into a loving relationship, which enlivens and makes sense of the dead stones of classical Rome. Everywhere, even in the shape of the rhetoric, opposites are held in creative balance. In the first elegy the touristic features of Rome form a dull list of stones, palazzi, streets and ramparts, but the prospect of sex, the paradoxical 'fire' that 'shall freshen', has a more exciting contrastive form. As sex turns to love, the reciprocity of the couple's relationship and the reciprocity of body and mind come together in an image of the couple in bed, he marking the rhythm of the elegiac couplet on her back as she sleeps, she breathing the hot breath of inspiration into his mouth. This balance of forces is held momentarily in suspension against the threat of lifelessness. In their awareness of death, the *Elegies* and the *Epigrams* are alike. But the *Epigrams* tell a story about casual sex in dirty, mercenary Venice. With bitterness the poet concedes that much of life is spent floating along in careless neglect of death. There are acid meditations on politics, money, and other weaknesses. The poetry has a quality of sharpness, but there is also sheer pleasure in the tangible realities of life and in the feeling that, although life is a game which we are bound to lose, we cannot help but enjoy it. In the end there is the consolation that even the most mechanical coupling is part of the process by which life is born.

Goethe's classical period includes poems to which the label classicism applies no better than it does to many poems of earlier and later phrases. It further confuses matters that German literary historians use the term '*Weimarer Klassik*' ('Weimar classical period') for the collaboration between Goethe and Friedrich Schiller (1759–1805) from 1794 until Schiller's death. Apart from its grandiose and unhelpful connotations of 'classic' status, the label has tended to understate the differences between the two writers, to the detriment of both. Schiller's natural medium was drama; Goethe's was the lyric and narrative poem. They collaborated well enough for it to be hard, in some lesser works, to see where one writer stops and the other begins, and they shared a set of literary values, amounting to a two-man campaign to reform German literature. (Similarities with the collaboration of Wordsworth and Coleridge do not stop there.) This joint venture in literary politics was as exposed and precarious as the balance of creative forces in the *Roman Elegies*. In any case, Goethe's classicism always had a different flavour from Schiller's. In the narrower sense, it meant 'living in' classical authors and assimilating their voices. This Goethe did with more success than any poet before or since, and the results are an extraordinary (and extraordinarily modern) mixture of authenticity and ventriloquism. The voice of the *Roman Elegies* is altogether ingenuous: personal, enthusiastic, playful, and knowingly male. But it cannot be heard without other poetic voices crowding in and reinforcing it in a chorus both alien and familiar. For the remainder of Goethe's life as a writer we catch echoes of Homer, Pindar, the Roman elegists, Virgil, the Greek anthology. Classical motifs which Goethe first made his own in the early 1770s – the traveller, the cycle of water from river to sea to cloud – are re-used with variations in the classical phase and later.

Classicism was also a set of values, which Schiller helped to formulate and to publicise in his journal *The Horai* (1794–98), named after the Greek goddesses of the seasons. Central to these was the appropriateness of poetic form and content to the rules of a genre. Goethe and Schiller believed that the classical genres were distinct because they each made different demands on audiences. Embedded in these genres were psychological norms. (This is one reason why Weimar classicism has seemed to English ears to be closer to Romanticism than, say, to the neo-classical Augustans, with their socially constructed notions of appropriateness; for Goethe and Schiller appropriateness implied naturalness and simplicity.) From this it followed that the genres had to be kept distinct, but that the stock of genres was not fixed, for new ones could be derived through reasoning about audience responses. Literary styles define themselves, among other things, by what they exclude. For instance, Goethe's classical writing, unless in comical mode, excludes 'low' topics such as food (except fruit) and drinks (except water and wine). More significantly and, for some readers, damagingly, the poems carefully renounce certain forms of emotion, in opposition first to *Empfindsamkeit*, then to Romanticism. Emotions are allowed that are appropriate to the formative experiences of love, frustration, jealousy, and loss. There is no room for the pseudo-emotion of guilt, which Goethe could not abide.

Some critics of Goethe's classicism have argued that it was fragile, that the poetry's surface calm, like the idyll of Le Petit Trianon, was won by excluding the modern revolutionary world. Certainly Goethe and Schiller believed that poetry had to be different from everyday politics, in the same way as one might say that history has to be different from journalism. There was no avoidance of politics in its broader, more reflective sense. During this difficult revolutionary time Goethe's poetry stayed close to its proper themes, themselves hardly unpolitical, of human beginnings and development. But Goethe returned to Weimar from Italy in 1788, the year before the French Revolution broke out. Classicism was born into political upheaval, and the 'classical decade' could not have been more inimical to poetry: it saw the Terror, the emergence of Napoleon, and the spread of war to most of western Europe. In Weimar the cultured society of the 1780s and '90s also passed, with the death of Herder in 1803, Schiller in 1805, and, in 1807, the Duke's mother Anna Amalia, patron of the 'Weimar Court of the Muses'. In 1806, after Napoleon's defeat of Prussia at the battle of Jena-Auerstedt, French forces marched into Weimar. Under such pressures, it has been argued, the fragility of classicism became manifest, and Goethe abandoned it. The years immediately after Schiller's death are usually taken as the start of a new phase in Goethe's writing. But the project of classicism could (and did) re-invent itself. Goethe's poetic repertoire extended to more modern though still traditional forms such as the sonnet, the *ottava rima*, and the *terza rima*. As well as being a poetry of human nature, classicism became a poetry of history. It found a new purpose in renewing traditional forms of European culture for a changing world. Goethe's frame of reference also widened to include more distant cultures. There is the *West-Östlicher Divan*, a cycle of poems inspired by the Persian poet Hafiz; the sequence of short poems, *Chinese-German Hours and Seasons*, inspired by Goethe's reading of Chinese poetry; and a strong interest in Greek pre-Socratic philosophy.

The Persian, Chinese, and early Greek models appealed to Goethe because they were untouched by the modern European split between poetry and science. Goethe could no more abide a poetry that was 'merely' art and therefore irrelevant, than he could a science that had lost the ability to express processes in nature without robbing them of the dynamism that was their essence. He adapted alien modes of poetry to give dynamic form to moments of creation and change, which prose could only resolve into slow-footed paradox. Poetry opened an escape from the literal-mindedness of scientific prose. From about 1790 to about 1810, Goethe worked on the science of light and colour. The resulting *Theory of Colour* (1810) consisted of three sections: a 'didactic' section on the experimental science, a 'polemical' section intended to dethrone the Newtonian orthodoxy, and, most interestingly, a 'historical' section on theories of colour since the pre-Socratics. For the most part Goethe's work was poorly received by the scientific community, and with good cause: the physics was naive, and the polemic against Newton self-destructive. The experience of failure forced Goethe to see himself as one not necessarily successful participant in the public discourse of science. And in a sense, the colour theory was designed to be received in this way. It did after all present itself, in the historical section, as one in a series of attempts at a seemingly insoluble problem. The philosophical epigrams – 'Unless the eye had sunlike parts', 'What God would nudge his world but not be in it' (pp. 107 and 119) – should be read with this sense of an unending scientific process in mind. These incursions into the discourse of science have a poetic form appropriate to the world of suspended oppositions they depict – a world containing God and contained by God, in which force is present in action and reaction – and to the endlessly controversial and changing nature of the scientific discourse with which they engage. Pairs of poems in this collection that seem flatly to contradict one another ('One and All' and 'Testament', pp. 133 and 151, or 'Epirrhema' and

'Antepirrhema', p. 127) are part of the process by which the modern discourse of science works. The poems are part of a changing world, capable of re-interpretation and revision.

The late poems testify to Goethe's capacity to stay true to his poetic gift by re-inventing himself. There are new themes, and old themes are revisited. Many of the later poems centre on friendship as a consolation in the face of death. The style is terse, and the technique is used whereby the poem is imagined as a fragment from a dialogue, spoken by a plausibly natural voice. Simple effects – here restrained diction, repetition, and a regular trochaic rhythm with strong mid-line caesura – are combined to evoke resignation:

Sag, was könnt uns Mandarinen,	Tell us mandarins enquiring,
Satt zu herrschen, müd zu dienen,	Sated rulers, servants tiring,
Sag, was könnt uns übrigbleiben,	Tell, what's left us except yearning
Als in solchen Frühlingstagen	To be quit when spring's around us,
Uns des Nordens zu entschlagen	Shaking off the North that bound us,
Und am Wasser und im Grünen	And by ponds, on grass reclining,
Fröhlich trinken, geistig schreiben,	Gaily drink, write wit and learning,
Schal auf Schale, Zug in Zügen?	Cup on cup, brushed strokes entwining?

Conventional religious assurances of the immortality of the soul did not work for Goethe. He did, though, re-interpret elements of Christian mythology in a way that accorded with his classical and naturalistic turn of mind. The grand mystical finale of *Faust II* is this kind of re-interpretation, as is the short poem 'Eve of St Nepomuk' (p. 129), celebrating a fourteenth-century Bohemian bishop who loyally kept the confidentiality of confession even in the face of death. The consolatory poems are successful re-inventions of a traditional mode. They work as consolations because they take fear seriously. The starkness of death is made obvious: a bleak sea-shore graveyard at night in a storm, a chaotic ossuary ('Memorial', p. 123; 'Schiller's Remains', p. 147). It is the ability to feel emptiness which is so threatening and which has to be conquered. If it is not – and that possibility is taken more seriously than some of Goethe's critics like to admit (see above all 'Trilogy of Passion', p. 135) – death will seep into life and suffocate it, as Werther showed. Consolation comes in two forms. There is the kind of consolation that poetry can give: the bringing together in poetry of intelligible sense and the physical beauty of sound as evidence that the conflicts in the world are soluble. There is also the disarming assurance, won by means of a patient openness to the world, that '*das Leben, es ist gut*' ('life is good'; 'The Bridegroom', p. 145).

Again the fear is that the feeling imagination which makes the world can also destroy it. The imagination must be prevented from turning in on itself and must be forced to open itself to the world. In the end, of course, consolation is all these poems offer: not a philosophical or theological demonstration, but a feeling of being lifted and buoyed by life, even if only briefly.

Goethe enjoyed seeing his writing translated and did not share the fastidious modern view that poetry is by its very nature untranslatable. But Goethe's poetry *is* particularly difficult to translate. In English, trochaic and classical quantitative metres are less natural, and feminine rhymes (*leben-geben*; *living-giving*) less frequent than in German. Add to that the short, four-foot lines in which Goethe often writes, and the translator has very little room for manoeuvre. The vocabulary and imagery is generally simple, but that can create its own problems, when the translator, perhaps trying to compensate for losing the feel of the poetry's rhythms, is tempted to write in an elevated or poeticised English which then misses the tension between naturalness and artifice that is so characteristic of Goethe's poetry. This introduction is fortunate to be able to break with the convention of complaining about the lack of good English translations of Goethe's poems. John Whaley gives a faithful rendition of the meaning and flavour of Goethe's poems. His Goethe is above all rhythmic. English-speaking readers who know Goethe's poems through musical settings will know how important rhythm is for them. They are poems which demand performance and a receptive ear. John Whaley's translations come as close to capturing the sound of Goethe's poems as English can.

   This selection includes examples of Goethe's best work from every decade of his writing life, in chronological order. It is designed to give the English-speaking reader an overview of Goethe's poetry. Readers who know Goethe's poems well will probably find that one or two of their favourites are not included. The selection could have been much longer without sacrificing quality. The aim here has been to give a representative selection of Goethe's poetry which does justice to its variety of forms, subjects and moods.

MATTHEW BELL

References

1. 'Goethe's profound and imperturbable naturalism was absolutely fatal to all routine thinking; he puts the standard, once for all, inside every man instead of outside him.' *Lectures and Essays in Criticism*, ed. R. H. Super (Ann Arbor: University of Michigan Press, 1962), p. 110.

2. '*Die Conzequenz der Natur tröstet schön über die Inconsequenz der Menschen*' (2 April 1785).

TRANSLATOR'S NOTE

Robert Frost once said that 'poetry' is 'what gets left out in translation', and that view is not uncommon. But many who hold to it do not necessarily make clear what they mean by the omitted 'poetry', still less agree on it with others who share that view. An over-riding concern for me in making these translations has been to counter that criticism as far as I can. And in order to do so it seems to me necessary to aim at preserving the clarity, and in some ways everyday nature, of Goethe's diction and its many varied moods, to follow his metrical patterns as far as possible, and to convey something of what nevertheless remains its special quality. That it might be possible to do so is a view that Goethe might well share, as the short poem 'An Equation' (p. 149) hints, when he says, on hearing a translation of one of his poems, that 'a marvel came to pass' as if the changed words 'still stood in their mother earth … marvellously strange in an alien tongue'.

Goethe highlighted three elements in the making of a poem – the *Stoff*, the *Gehalt*, and the *Form*. *Stoff* is the subject matter taken from everyday experience. The *Gehalt*, literally 'content', is the particular interpretation of that subject matter, the theme introduced into it by the poet's own 'rich inner nature'. The *Form* of a poem 'must be well thought through'. It is that which has to do with making a poem something more than, and yet consistent with, the subject matter and its import. The appropriate metre is part of it.

There are poems in Goethe's lyric cycle, the *West-Östlicher Divan*[1], which expressly testify to the impact of rhyme and the importance he attached to it. And it certainly seems clear that he considered metrics and

---

[1] This selection of Goethe's poems contains none from the substantial lyric cycle known as the *West-Östlicher Divan* because a translation of the entire cycle (a third, revised edition) is being published as a separate volume.

rhyme to be crucial and indispensable to his own poetry. It is in this area of
metre and rhyme that I have seen the keenest debate amongst translators
and professional critics. At one extreme a critic, who himself translated
Faust in a prose version, declared roundly that 'proximity to the meaning
of the German and apt English idiom are the two, and sufficient,
principles for the translation of Goethe's verse' and that 'the meaning is in
the meaning'. On this basis he reproached Louis MacNeice for choosing
rhyme as the vehicle for his translation of *Faust*. But that criticism evades
the question of what is to be done if some of the meaning should be in the
very existence of rhyme. Or as MacNeice put it, 'the rhymes in Goethe are
part of the sense and [Goethe] uses them again and again to clinch his
point'. There are many examples in Goethe's lyric work which substan-
tiate MacNeice's view and in some cases express it directly and
conceptually. For example, in a poem from the *Divan* in praise and
imitation of the Persian poet Hafiz he says, deliberately imitating the
sometimes monotonous poetic form of the Persian Ode, the *ghasel*:

> To your own style of rhyme I'm now inclining,
> In repetitions I shall be delighting,
> To sense then words their proper place assigning:
> I'll find no sound a second time inviting
> Unless thereby the meaning it's refining
> As, gifted one, in all your peerless writing.

Perhaps the greatest, and most well known, demonstration of this
viewpoint is when Goethe uses rhyme to bring about a synthesis of the
modern and the classical cultures at the wedding of Faust to Helen in
Faust Part II. This process is playfully mirrored in the *West-Östlicher
Divan* when the Houri courteously chooses to give Goethe a guide to
Paradise in the doggerel rhyming of Hans Sachs so as to make him feel
more at home.

   Although it impoverishes the reading of Goethe to think that rhyme
does not matter, the translator nevertheless has to face the challenge in the
argument that he should refrain from rhyming because 'you can't make
rhymes without sacrificing sense to sound'. The translator must try to
avoid the sacrifice of sense, knowing that he can fail because he does the
original to death either by starving it of meaning or by choking it under
extraneous matter added by his own rhymes. The translator must, then,
tread carefully and do his best to negotiate between this Scylla and
Charybdis by careful control of the content of his own rhyming. He must
do so because, in my view, the attempt at rhyme is crucial to an adequate
rendering of Goethe's poetry. In making that attempt he will recognise

with regret that English is poorer than German in its capacity to generate sustained weak feminine (ending with an unstressed syllable) rhymes and line endings. This is largely because English nowadays has retained fewer inflections than German, which still maintains a large body of inflection in its conjugations of verbs and declensions of nouns. Thus, for example, the trochaic metre (one stressed followed by one unstressed syllable) is no longer as available to the English poet, whereas in German verse it enjoys equal status with the iambic measure (one unstressed followed by one stressed syllable) familiar to English poetry. There are certainly far too many occasions where it proves not at all possible for the translator to find suitable feminine rhymes and line endings in English. But I believe that the opportunities are greater than often seems recognised. And I have not so far seen any basis for thinking that feminine rhyme and line endings are alien to the spirit of English. It is, of course, even more difficult to find and sustain acceptable feminine endings for long hendecasyllabic (eleven syllable) lines within a strict formal rhyme pattern where all the rhymes are feminine, such as the *ottava rima* which Goethe uses for 'The Diary' (p. 107), and the *terza rima* of the poem sometimes called 'Schiller's Remains' (p. 147). The translations of those poems, and of the seventeen Sonnets (p. 89) and 'Wilhelm Tischbein's Idylls' (p. 129), are exclusively feminine-rhyming. They, and others where feminine rhymes are prominent (such as 'Why give us deep vision . . . ?' (p. 33), 'Lasting Change' (p. 85), 'To the Moon' (p. 55), 'Dedication' (p. 49), and 'At Midnight' (p. 125), show, I believe, that it is not always impossible to model Goethe's stress and rhyme patterns in English verse.

My remarks have centred on the question for the translator of translating rhyme and metrical pattern. But it should be remembered that the poet of the originating language has similarly to contend with the whole of its nature, which will have its advantages and its deficiencies. With its inflections German allows more numerous rhyming possibilities and greater flexibility in positioning words in the lines, because the sequence of words in the sentences does not determine the sense so much as it does in English. This greater flexibility allows a master craftsman such as Goethe, as he tells us in a poem from the *West-Östlicher Divan*, to feel that the poet can 'swim about' in the language as if in water and 'manipulate it' as can a sculptor modelling clay. But he too feels the constraints along with the advantages. Sonnets XI, XIV, and XV (pp. 99, 101 and 103) address the inspirational effect and advantages of a sophisticated rigorous poetic form such as the sonnet; but they do so without in any way denying the burden also entailed as the poet pushes forward with crafting it, only to encounter repeated complications like

Sisyphus pushing 'the stone uphill in steps so tiring/Whilst back it rolls and makes the struggle harder'. The translator fares similarly. In his case, as well as tackling the problems of sound patterns, he needs to recognise what scholars have established as the highly charged nature, for Goethe, of simple words such as *trüb* (dark, dismal, troubled, and the like) and *rein* (clean, clear, pure, etc.) and to render them aptly in their varying contexts. He has to fathom the real meaning of the words and phrases, and decide what to do about ambiguities in the German (ought they to be retained in the English?); should one try to emulate Goethe's neologisms? – and so on, endlessly. With an author like Goethe who could say that 'if a dictionary can keep pace with an author he's no good' (*Maxims and Reflections*, No. 916), the translator might well groan at the effort to push his stone uphill and even be tempted to feel that the original author may have had an easier ride! But his compensation is to gain a richer awareness of both languages and the pleasure of a closer knowledge of the works he translates. But these are by-products. Goethe said that translators are 'zealous procurers ... arousing an irresistible inclination towards the original' (*Maxims and Reflections*, No. 947). English speakers deserve a resonable opportunity to know as much as possible of the preoccupations, qualities and flavour of the poetry of Germany's greatest poet. I hope these translations will go some way towards providing that opportunity.

For the translation of this selection of Goethe's poetry I owe a very large debt to Jim Reed, who gave liberally of his time and offered numerous – but always constructive – criticisms (and suggestions how to find a way round so many of them). I am also indebted to Katharina Mommsen, who has supported me with friendly and enthusiastic comment in all my translation work and given me the benefits of her great scholarship. Lastly, I am also very grateful to Matthew Bell for his Introduction to the poems from which I have learned so much.

JOHN WHALEY

Vom Vater hab ich die Statur,
Des Lebens ernstes Führen;
Vom Mütterchen die Frohnatur
Und Lust zu fabulieren.

My stature is my Father's part,
Life's earnest from the cradle;
From Mother I've my sunny heart
And fancy for a fable.

From *Friendly Xenia* VI

CHRONOLOGY OF GOETHE'S LIFE

Year	Age	Life
1749		Born 28 August in Frankfurt-am-Main to Johann Caspar and Catharina Elisabeth (née Textor)
1750		Sister Cornelia born
1751	1	
1753	2	Grandmother gives Goethe puppet-theatre for Christmas
1755	5	Renovation of Goethe family home
1756	6	Begins to learn Latin and Greek
1759	9	
1760	10	
1762	12	
1763	13	
1764	14	
1765	15	Leaves for Leipzig to study law
1766	16	
1767	17	
1768	18	Serious illness and return to Frankfurt

CHRONOLOGY OF HIS TIMES

Year	Literary Context	Historical Events
1749	Buffon, *Histoire naturelle* (to 1788)	
1750		Witch-trials abolished in Prussia
1751	Publication of the *Encyclopedia* (Diderot et al.) begins (to 1772)	
1755	Lessing, *Miss Sara Sampson*	Lisbon earthquake
1756		Seven Years' War (to 1763)
1759	Schiller born Voltaire, *Candide*	
1760	McPherson, *Fragments of Ancient Poetry* ('Ossian') Rousseau, *La Nouvelle Héloïse*	
1762	Wieland's translations of Shakespeare (to 1766) Rousseau, *Emile* and *The Social Contract*	
1763	Winckelmann, *History of the Art of Antiquity*	
1764		Coronation of Joseph II as Holy Roman Emperor in Frankfurt Proscription of Jesuit order in France
1766	Goldsmith, *The Vicar of Wakefield*	
1767	Lessing, *Minna von Barnhelm* and *Hamburg Dramaturgy* (to 1768) Wieland, *History of Agathon*	
1768	Winckelmann dies Sterne, *Sentimental Journey* Gerstenberg, *Ugolino*	

Year	Age	Life
1769	19	Interest in Pietism
		First collection of poems published
1770	20	In Strasbourg to finish law studies
		Meets Herder and collects Alsatian popular songs
1771	21	Awarded law doctorate
		Götz von Berlichingen (published 1773)
1772	22	At Imperial Law Courts in Wetzlar
1773	23	Cornelia marries
1774	24	*The Sufferings of Young Werther*; *Faust* begun
1775	25	Engagement to Lili Schönemann (broken off in October)
		Travels in Switzerland
		Moves to Weimar on the invitation of Duke Karl August
1776	26	Friendship with Charlotte von Stein
		Interest in geology
		Begins *Wilhelm Meister*
1777	27	Cornelia dies
		Travels in the Harz
1778	28	
1779	29	Travels in Switzerland
		Iphigenia in Tauris (prose version)
1780	30	Becomes Freemason
1781	31	
1782	32	Ennoblement
1784	34	Discovers *os intermaxillare* in humans
		Launches Mongolfier hot air balloon in Weimar
1785	35	
1786	36	Leaves for Rome, via Verona and Venice
1787	37	To Naples and Sicily
1788	38	Returns to Weimar
		Begins living with Christiane Vulpius
1789	39	Son August born
		Torquato Tasso
		Essay *On the Metamorphosis of Plants*

Year	Literary Context	Historical Events
1769	Wood, *Essay on the Original Genius of Homer*	Napoleon born
1770	Hölderlin, Wordsworth and Beethoven born	
1772	Coleridge born Lessing, *Emilia Galotti* Herder, *Treatise on the Origin of Language*	
1775	Lavater, *Physiognomic Fragments* (to 1778)	
1776	Adam Smith, *The Wealth of Nations* Lenz, *The Soldiers* Klinger, *The Twins* Kleist born	US Declaration of Independence
1778	Voltaire and Rousseau die Lessing, *Nathan the Wise*	
1780		Judicial torture abolished in France
1781	Lessing dies Schiller, *The Robbers* Kant, *Critique of Pure Reason*	
1784	Diderot dies Herder, *Ideas on the Philosophy of the History of Mankind*	
1785		Diamond Necklace Affair
1786	Mozart, *The Marriage of Figaro*	Frederick the Great dies
1788	Byron born Kant, *Critique of Practical Reason*	Convocation of French States-General
1789	Mozart, *Così fan tutte*	French Revolution begins Storming of the Bastille

Year	Age	Life
1790	40	Travels to Venice
		Venetian Epigrams (published 1796)
		Faust. A Fragment.
1791	41	Study of optics
1792	42	Accompanies Duke Karl August on campaign against France
1793	43	Present at the siege of Mainz
1794	44	Friendship with Schiller
1795	45	*Roman Elegies*
		Wilhelm Meister's Apprenticeship published (to 1796)
1796	46	
1797	47	*Hermann and Dorothea*
		Begins work on *Faust* again
		Travels in Switzerland
1798	48	'Year of Ballads'
1799	49	
1800	50	Translations of Voltaire's plays
1801	51	*Faust I* substantially finished
1802	52	
1803	53	Mme de Staël and Benjamin Constant in Weimar (to 1804)
1804	54	

Year	Literary Context	Historical Events
1790	Kant, *Critique of Judgement*	Abolition of the nobility and civil constitution of the clergy in France Joseph II dies
1791	Mozart, *The Magic Flute* Mozart dies	
1792	Rossini born	Louis XVI deposed Alliance of Austria and Prussia against France Cannonade of Valmy
1793		The Terror Execution of Louis XVI
1794	Fichte, *Theory of Science*	Execution of Robespierre
1795	Schiller, *On the Aesthetic Education of Man* Wolf, *Prolegomena ad Homerum* Keats born	Treaty of Basle
1796	Schiller, *On Naive and Sentimental Poetry* Hufeland, *Macrobiotics*	
1797	Hölderlin, *Hyperion* Schelling, *Philosophy of Nature* Heine, Schubert born	
1798	Schiller, *Wallenstein* trilogy first performed in Weimar	French troops occupy Rome Napoleon in Egypt
	Wordsworth and Coleridge, *Lyrical Ballads*	Battle of the Nile
1799	Novalis, *Christendom, or Europe*	Second coalition against France Napoleon becomes First Consul
1800	Schelling, *System of Transcendental Idealism* Schiller, *Mary Stuart*	
1801	Schiller, *The Maid of Orleans* Novalis dies	
1802	Dumas and Hugo born	Peace of Amiens
1803	Schiller, *The Bride of Messina* Herder dies Klopstock dies	
1804	Schiller, *William Tell* Kant dies	Napoleon crowned Emperor

Year	Age	Life
1805	55	*Winckelmann and his Century*
1806	56	French troops occupy Weimar
		Goethe and Christiane Vulpius are married
1807	57	Duchess Anna Amalia, mother of Duke Karl August, dies
1808	58	Publication of *Faust I*
		Meets Napoleon at Erfurt
1809	59	*The Elective Affinities*
		Pandora
1810	60	*Theory of Colour*
1811	61	*Poetry and Truth* (to 1814)
1812	62	Meets Beethoven in Teplitz
1813	63	
1814	64	Starts poems in the manner of Hafiz
1815	65	
1816	66	*Italian Journey* (to 1817)
		Christiane dies
1817	67	
1819	69	*West-Eastern Divan*
1821	71	*Wilhelm Meister's Journeyman Years*
1824	74	
1825	75	
1827	77	
1828	78	Duke Karl August dies
1829	79	First public performance of *Faust I*, in Braunschweig
1830	80	Goethe's only surviving child,
		August, dies in Rome
		Chinese-German Hours and Seasons
1831	81	
1832	82	Goethe dies on 22 March
		Faust II published

Year	Literary Context	Historical Events
1805	Schiller dies	Third coalition against France Battles of Trafalgar and Austerlitz
1806	Arnim and Brentano, *The Boy's Magic Horn*, vol. 1 (dedicated to Goethe)	Battles of Jena and Auerstedt Capitulation of Prussia Holy Roman Empire ceases to exist
1807	Hegel, *Phenomenology of Mind*	Peace of Tilsit
1809	Darwin born	
1811	Kleist dies	
1812	Grimm, *Fairy Tales* J. von Hammer's translation of Hafiz' *Divan* (to 1814)	Napoleon's Russian campaign
1813	Wieland dies Verdi and Wagner born	
1814		Bonaparte exiled to Elba
1815		The Hundred Days Battle of Waterloo
1816	Clausewitz, *On War* Rossini, *The Barber of Seville*	
1817	Byron, *Manfred*	
1819	Schopenhauer, *The World as Will and Imagination* Mary Ann Evans (George Eliot) born	
1821		Greek uprising against Turkish rule
1824	Byron dies	
1825	Manzoni, *The Betrothed*	
1827	Heine, *Book of Songs*	
1831	Hegel dies	

GOETHE
SELECTED POEMS

Maifest

Wie herrlich leuchtet
Mir die Natur!
Wie glänzt die Sonne!
Wie lacht die Flur!

Es dringen Blüten   5
Aus jedem Zweig
Und tausend Stimmen
Aus dem Gesträuch

Und Freud und Wonne
Aus jeder Brust.   10
O Erd', o Sonne,
O Glück, o Lust,

O Lieb', o Liebe,
So golden schön
Wie Morgenwolken   15
Auf jenen Höhn,

Du segnest herrlich
Das frische Feld,
Im Blütendampfe
Die volle Welt!   20

O Mädchen, Mädchen,
Wie lieb' ich dich!
Wie blinkt dein Auge,
Wie liebst du mich!

So liebt die Lerche   25
Gesang und Luft,
Und Morgenblumen
Den Himmelsduft,

Wie ich dich liebe
Mit warmen Blut,   30
Die du mir Jugend
Und Freud' und Mut

Zu neuen Liedern
Und Tänzen gibst.
Sei ewig glücklich,   35
Wie du mich liebst.

May Song *(March 1771)*

How splendid nature
Shines all for me!
The sun, it sparkles!
Fields laugh with glee!

From all the branches   5
The blossoms push,
A thousand voices
From every bush

And joy and rapture
From every breast.   10
O earth, o sunshine,
O bliss, o zest,

O love, o love,
So golden bright
As clouds of morning   15
Upon that height,

On fresh fields richly
Your blessings spill,
With haze of blossom
The world you fill!   20

O girl my darling
How I love you!
Your eyes, how shining!
How you love too!

So loves the skylark   25
Its song on high
And morning flowers
The fragrant sky

As I am burning
With love for you   30
Who give me courage
And youth anew,

Give joy, set singing
And dancing free;
Be ever happy   35
As you love me.

Willkommen und Abschied

Es schlug mein Herz. Geschwind, zu Pferde!
Und fort, wild wie ein Held zur Schlacht.
Der Abend wiegte schon die Erde,
Und an den Bergen hing die Nacht.
Schon stund im Nebelkleid die Eiche   5
Wie ein getürmter Riese da,
Wo Finsternis aus dem Gesträuche
Mit hundert schwarzen Augen sah.

Der Mond von einem Wolkenhügel
Sah schläfrig aus dem Duft hervor,   10
Die Winde schwangen leise Flügel,
Umsausten schauerlich mein Ohr.
Die Nacht schuf tausend Ungeheuer,
Doch tausendfacher war mein Mut,
Mein Geist war ein verzehrend Feuer,   15
Mein ganzes Herz zerfloß in Glut.

Ich sah dich, und die milde Freude
Floß aus dem süßen Blick auf mich.
Ganz war mein Herz an deiner Seite,
Und jeder Atemzug für dich.   20
Ein rosenfarbes Frühlingswetter
Lag auf dem lieblichen Gesicht
Und Zärtlichkeit für mich, ihr Götter,
Ich hofft' es, ich verdient' es nicht.

Der Abschied, wie bedrängt, wie trübe!   25
Aus deinen Blicken sprach dein Herz.
In deinen Küssen welche Liebe,
O welche Wonne, welcher Schmerz!
Du gingst, ich stund und sah zur Erden
Und sah dir nach mit nassem Blick.   30
Und doch, welch Glück, geliebt zu werden,
Und lieben, Götter, welch ein Glück!

Meeting and Parting (Spring 1771)

My heart beat wild. And off, like lightning!
I rode as if to meet the foe.
In evening cradled earth was quietening
And on the hills the night hung low.
In cloak of mist the oak tree towered,   5
Rearing like a giant there
Where darkness from the bushes glowered
With all a hundred eyes' black stare.

On high-banked clouds the moon was peering
From out the haze with sleepy eyes,   10
The winds on quiet wings were veering
And passed me by with awesome sighs.
Though night spawned monstrous thousands lowering
A thousandfold more bold I stood,
My spirit was a flame devouring   15
And all my heart a burning flood.

I saw you, and the gentling sweetness
Flowed over me with each look from you.
Whole was my heart, you brought completeness,
For you was every breath I drew.   20
A rosy hue of springtime's season
Coloured that dearest lovely face
And tenderness for me, beyond reason,
Ye gods, I'd hoped, not earned, such grace.

The parting, how oppressed, how troubled!   25
Your looks spoke all your heart again.
In all your kisses love redoubled!
How great the bliss, how great the pain!
You went, downcast I stood unmoving
And followed you with moistening eyes.   30
And yet, what prize to win such loving,
To love, oh gods, oh what a prize!

Mahomets-Gesang

Seht den Felsenquell
Freudehell,
Wie ein Sternenblick!
Über Wolken
Nährten seine Jugend   5
Gute Geister
Zwischen Klippen im Gebüsch.

Jünglingfrisch
Tanzt er aus der Wolke
Auf die Marmorfelsen nieder,   10
Jauchzet wieder
Nach dem Himmel.

Durch die Gipfelgänge
Jagt er bunten Kieseln nach,
Und mit frühem Führertritt   15
Reißt er seine Bruderquellen
Mit sich fort.

Drunten werden in dem Tal
Unter seinem Fußtritt Blumen,
Und die Wiese   20
Lebt von seinem Hauch.

Doch ihn hält kein Schattental,
Keine Blumen,
Die ihm seine Knie' umschlingen,
Ihm mit Liebesaugen schmeicheln;   25
Nach der Ebne dringt sein Lauf,
Schlangewandelnd.

Bäche schmiegen
Sich gesellig an.
Nun tritt er   30
In die Ebne silberprangend,
Und die Ebne prangt mit ihm,
Und die Flüsse von der Ebne
Und die Bäche von Gebürgen
Jauchzen ihm und rufen: Bruder,   35
Bruder, nimm die Brüder mit,
Mit zu deinem alten Vater,

Mohammed's Song (1772–3)

See the spring in the cliff
Bright with joy
Like the radiance of stars!
Over clouds
Its youth was nurtured   5
By good spirits
In the cliffs and scrub.

Youthful freshly
It dances from the cloud
Down to the marble cliffs below,   10
Jubilating
To the heavens.

Through the summit passes
It chases after the bright pebbles
And it strides as a young leader   15
Pulling its brother wellsprings
Along with it.

Down in the valley
Flowers come where it steps,
And the meadow   20
Lives from its breath.

But no shadowed valley can keep him,
Nor no flowers
Winding around his knees,
Flattering him with the eyes of love;   25
To the plain his course drives on,
Snakelike sliding.

Brooks sidle
Companionly.
Now he steps   30
On the plain resplendently silvered,
And the plain's resplendent with him,
And the rivers from the lowlands
And the brooklets from the mountains
Jubilate and cry out; brother,   35
Brother, take your brothers with you,
To your age-old father,

Zu dem ew'gen Ozean,
Der mit weitverbreit'ten Armen
Unsrer wartet;   40
Die sich, ach, vergebens öffnen,
Seine Sehnenden zu fassen;
Denn uns frißt in öder Wüste
Gier'ger Sand,

Die Sonne droben   45
Saugt an unserm Blut,
Ein Hügel
Hemmet uns zum Teiche.
Bruder,
Nimm die Brüder von der Ebne,   50
Nimm die Brüder von Gebürgen
Mit, zu deinem Vater mit!

Kommt ihr alle! –
Und nun schwillt er
Herrlicher, ein ganz Geschlechte   55
Trägt den Fürsten hoch empor,
Und im rollenden Triumphe
Gibt er Ländern Namen, Städte
Werden unter seinem Fuß.

Unaufhaltsam rauscht er über,   60
Läßt der Türme Flammengipfel,
Marmorhäuser, eine Schöpfung
Seiner Fülle, hinter sich.

Zedernhäuser trägt der Atlas
Auf den Riesenschultern, sausend   65
Wehen über seinem Haupte
Tausend Segel auf zum Himmel
Seine Macht und Herrlichkeit.

Und so trägt er seine Brüder,
Seine Schätze, seine Kinder   70
Dem erwartenden Erzeuger
Freudebrausend an das Herz.

To the eternal ocean
Where with outspread arms
Us it waits for;   40
Arms, alas, which open vainly
For the ones who're yearning for him;
For we're devoured in the barren desert
By greedy sand,

The sun up there   45
Sucks our blood,
A hillside
Hems us in as a pond.
Brother,
Take your brothers from the plains,   50
Take your brothers from the mountains
With you, with you to your father!

Come now all of you! –
And he swells up
More resplendent, all a tribe   55
Carries a prince aloft,
And rolling in triumph
He gives name to countries, cities
Spring up from his footsteps.

On he rushes irresistible,   60
Leaves the towers of flame-topped summits,
Marble houses, all created
By his abundance, all he leaves.

Cedar houses Atlas carries
On his giant shoulders, rippling   65
Sails that stream high up above him
Form a thousand confirmations
Of his power and his splendour.

Thus he carries all his brothers,
All his treasures and his children,   70
Foaming joyfully to the waiting
Heart of their progenitor.

Satyros
oder
Der vergötterte Waldteufel

Erster Akt (Auszug)

EINSIEDLER. Ihr denkt, ihr Herrn, ich bin allein,
Weil ich nicht mag in Städten sein.
Ihr irrt euch, liebe Herren mein!
Ich hab mich nicht hierher begeben,
Weil sie in Städten so ruchlos leben   5
Und alle wandeln nach ihrem Trieb,
Der Schmeichler, Heuchler und der Dieb:
Das hätt mich immerfort ergetzt,
Wollten sie nur nicht sein hochgeschätzt,
Bestehlen und be – mich, wie die Raben,   10
Und noch dazu Reverenzen haben!
Ihrer langweiligen Narrheit satt,
Bin herausgezogen in Gottes Stadt;
Wo's freilich auch geht drüber und drunter
Und geht demohngeacht nicht unter.   15
Ich sah im Frühling ohne Zahl
Blüten und Knospen durch Berg und Tal,
Wie alles drängt und alles treibt,
Kein Pläcklein ohne Keimlein bleibt.
Da denkt nun gleich der steif Philister: 20
Das ist für mich und meine Geschwister.
Unser Herrgott ist so gnädig heuer;
Hätt ich's doch schon in Fach und Scheuer!
Unser Herrgott spricht: Aber mir nit so;
Es sollen's ander auch werden froh.   25
Da lockt uns denn der Sonnenschein
Störch und Schwalb aus der Fremd herein,
Den Schmetterling aus seinem Haus,
Die Fliegen aus den Ritzen 'raus,
Und brütet das Raupenvölklein aus.   30
Das quillt all von Erzeugungskraft,
Wie sich's hat aus dem Schlaf gerafft;
Vögel und Frösch und Tier' und Mücken
Begehn sich zu allen Augenblicken,
Hinten und vorn, auf Bauch und Rücken,   35
Daß man auf jeder Blüt und Blatt

Satyros
or
The Idolized Demon of the Woods[1] (Autumn 1773)

From Act One

HERMIT. You think, dear Sirs, I've stepped aside
As life in towns I can't abide.
You're wrong though, all your guesses wide!
I didn't come here to the rabbits
Because the towns have shameful habits   5
And everyone by impulse plays
In false and fawning thievish ways:
All that had quite amusing seemed
Had they not sought to be esteemed,
To rob and shit on me undaunted,   10
And bows and scrapes as well they wanted!
Their tiresome clowning made me spew,
So here to God's City I withdrew;
Here too there's lots of rough and tumble
But nevertheless this one won't crumble.   15
I saw in spring the countless fill
Of buds and blooms through vale and hill,
How all's a thrusting driving need,
No peck of earth without its seed.
Then thinks the wooden Philistine: 20
All that is there for me and mine.
How kind today is God our Father;
In cupboard and barn it should be rather!
Our Lord God speaks: Not so, not true;
There's others who need to enjoy it too.   25
Then come enticed when sunshine starts
Storks and swallow from foreign parts,
From out its house the butterfly,
The flies from cracks wherein they lie,
And all the little larvae hatch out dry.   30
All that swells with the urge to beget
When it's freed itself from its sleepy net;
Midges, beasts, birds, frogs a-jumping,
Indulge every moment, bumping and thumping,
Backside and front, bellying and rumping,   35
So every flower and leaf they tread

Ein Eh- und Wochenbettlein hat.
Und sing ich dann im Herzen mein
Lob Gott mit allen Würmelein.
Das Volk will dann zu essen haben, 40
Verzehren bescherte Gottesgaben.
So frißt's Würmlein frisch Keimlein-Blatt,
Das Würmlein macht das Lerchlein satt,
Und weil ich auch bin zu essen hier,
Mir das Lerchlein zu Gemüte führ. 45
Ich bin denn auch ein häuslich Mann,
Hab Haus und Stall und Garten dran.
Mein Gärtlein, Früchtlein ich beschütz
Vor Kält und Raupen und dürrer Hitz.
Kommt aber herein der Kieselschlag 50
Und furaschiert mir an einem Tag,
So ärgert mich dèr Streich fürwahr;
Doch leb ich noch am End vom Jahr,
Wo mancher Werwolf ist schon tot
Aus Ängsten vor der Hungersnot. 55

Vierter Akt (Auszug)

SATYROS. Und bereitet zu dem tiefen Gang
Aller Erkenntnis, horchet meinem Gesang!
Vernehmt, wie im Unding 290
Alles durcheinander ging;
Im verschloßnen Haß die Elemente tosend,
Und Kraft an Kräften widrig von sich stoßend,
Ohne Feindsband, ohne Freundsband,
Ohne Zerstören, ohne Vermehren. 295
DAS VOLK. Lehr uns, wir hören!
SATYROS. Wie im Unding das Urding erquoll,
Lichtsmacht durch die Nacht scholl,
Durchdrang die Tiefen der Wesen all,
Daß aufkeimte Begehrungsschwall 300
Und die Elemente sich erschlossen,
Mit Hunger ineinander ergossen,
Alldurchdringend, alldurchdrungen.
HERMEMS. Des Mannes Geist ist von Göttern entsprungen.
SATYROS. Wie sich Haß und Lieb gebar 305
Und das All nun ein Ganzes war,
Und das Ganze klang

Is a bridal and confinement bed.
And then my heart leaps up and sings
Praise God with worms and little things.
The crowd then wants to eat and be sated, 40
Devour the gifts by God donated.
So wormlet eats fresh leafy bud,
On wormlet lark feels full and good,
And as I too have an eating part
The little lark I take to heart. 45
For I'm a really domestic man,
Keep house, stable, garden as well as I can.
My garden, my fruit I guard as meet
From cold, from crawlers, from drought and heat.
But if the hailstones come my way 50
And forage my stuff away in a day
I grant their trick makes me tear my hair;
But when each year ends I'm still there
Though many a werewolf's already dead
Because it suffered hunger's dread. 55

From Act Four

SATYROS. Get ready for the journey deep and long
To gain all knowledge, listen to my song!
Hear, how the Non-Thing 290
Had everything confused in a turmoiled ring,
In their pent-up hatred elements out-welling,
And force against forces each other repelling,
No foe joining, no friend joining,
Neither destroying, nor increasing! 295
PEOPLE. Teach us, your lesson's pleasing!
SATYROS. Hear, from the Non-Thing the Prime-Thing sprang out,
Through the night light's power rang out
Piercing all beings' depths with fire,
So germinated torrential desire 300
And the elements all exploded
In spate to mix by their hunger goaded,
All-penetrating, all penetrated.
HERMES. This man's spirit by gods was generated.
SATYROS. Hear, the birth of love and hate 305
Did from the All a Whole create,
And the Whole did resound

In lebend wirkendem Ebengesang,
Sich täte Kraft in Kraft verzehren,
Sich täte Kraft in Kraft vermehren,   310
Und auf und ab sich rollend ging
Das all und ein und ewig Ding,
Immer verändert, immer beständig!

Ganymed

Wie im Morgenrot
Du rings mich anglühst,
Frühling, Geliebter!
Mit tausendfacher Liebeswonne
Sich an mein Herz drängt   5
Deiner ewigen Wärme
Heilig Gefühl,
Unendliche Schöne!

Daß ich dich fassen möcht'
In diesen Arm!   10

Ach, an deinem Busen
Lieg' ich, schmachte,
Und deine Blumen, dein Gras
Drängen sich an mein Herz.
Du kühlst den brennenden   15
Durst meines Busens,
Lieblicher Morgenwind,
Ruft drein die Nachtigall
Liebend nach mir aus dem Nebeltal.

Ich komme! Ich komme!   20
Wohin? Ach, wohin?

Hinauf, hinauf strebt's,
Es schweben die Wolken
Abwärts, die Wolken
Neigen sich der sehnenden Liebe,   25
Mir, mir!
In eurem Schoße
Aufwärts,
Umfangend umfangen!

In living harmony working all round,
And force went at force in feeding,
And force went at force in breeding,   310
And up and down it rolled its ring,
That all and one and lasting Thing,
Forever changing, forever persisting!

Ganymede (*Spring 1774*)

How in the morning dawn
You glow all round me,
Springtime, beloved!
With love's blisses a-thousandfold
The sacred feeling   5
Of your eternal warmth
Pushes to my heart,
Infinite lovely one!

Could I but grasp you
Within this arm!   10

Oh, on your breast
I lie, languish,
And your flowers, your grass,
Thrust themselves at my heart.
You cool the burning   15
Thirst of my bosom,
Lovely breeze of the morning,
Through it the nightingale calls
Lovingly for me from the misty valley.

I come! I come!   20
To where? Oh, to where?

Upwards, upwards the urge,
The clouds are floating
Downwards, the clouds
Lower themselves towards yearning love,   25
To me, me!
In your lap
Upwards,
Embracing embraced!

Aufwärts   30
An deinem Busen,
Alliebender Vater!

Der neue Amadis

Als ich noch ein Knabe war,
Sperrte man mich ein,
Und so saß ich manches Jahr
Über mir allein
Wie in Mutterleib.   5

Doch du warst mein Zeitvertreib,
Goldne Phantasie,
Und ich ward ein warmer Held,
Wie der Prinz Pipi,
Und durchzog die Welt.   10

Baute manch kristallen Schloß
Und zerstört' es auch,
Warf mein blinkendes Geschoß
Drachen durch den Bauch,
Ja, ich war ein Mann!   15

Ritterlich befreit' ich dann
Die Prinzessin Fisch;
Sie war gar zu obligeant,
Führte mich zu Tisch,
Und ich war galant.   20

Und ihr Kuß war Himmelsbrot,
Glühend wie der Wein.
Ach, ich liebte fast mich tot,
Rings mit Sonnenschein
War sie emailliert.   25

Ach! Wer hat sie mir entführt?
Hielt kein Zauberband
Ihr verrät'risch Fliehn?
Sagt, wo ist ihr Land,
Wo der Weg dahin?   30

Upwards   30
Upon your breast,
All-loving father!

The New Amadis[2] (1774)

As a boy they locked me in,
Years spent on my own,
So I sat with time to spin
With myself alone
Just as in the womb.   5

But you helped and filled my room,
Golden fantasy,
And I had a hero's rage
Like the Prince Pipi,
All the world my stage.   10

Crystal castles I would build
And destroy them too,
Dragons' blood my fierce thrusts spilled,
Pierced their entrails through,
Yes, I was a man!   15

Then I freed, as true knights can,
Princess Fish of fable;
She was more than obligeant,
Led me to her table,
And I was galant.   20

And her kiss was Heaven's bread,
Glowing like the wine,
Oh! I loved till nearly dead
Whilst round her the sun did shine
Painted in gold leaf.   25

Oh, who took her, who the thief?
Could no magic band
Her false flight gainsay?
Tell me, where now is her land,
How to find the way?   30

Prometheus

Bedecke deinen Himmel, Zeus,
Mit Wolkendunst!
Und übe, Knaben gleich,
Der Disteln köpft,
An Eichen dich und Bergeshöhn! 5
Mußt mir meine Erde
Doch lassen stehn,
Und meine Hütte,
Die du nicht gebaut,
Und meinen Herd, 10
Um dessen Glut
Du mich beneidest.

Ich kenne nichts Ärmer's
Unter der Sonn' als euch Götter.
Ihr nähret kümmerlich 15
Von Opfersteuern
Und Gebetshauch
Eure Majestät
Und darbtet, wären
Nicht Kinder und Bettler 20
Hoffnungsvolle Toren.

Da ich ein Kind war,
Nicht wußt', wo aus, wo ein,
Kehrte mein verirrtes Aug'
Zur Sonne, als wenn drüber wär' 25
Ein Ohr, zu hören meine Klage,
Ein Herz wie meins,
Sich des Bedrängten zu erbarmen.

Wer half mir wider
Der Titanen Übermut? 30
Wer rettete vom Tode mich,
Von Sklaverei?
Hast du's nicht alles selbst vollendet,
Heilig glühend Herz?
Und glühtest, jung und gut, 35
Betrogen, Rettungsdank
Dem Schlafenden da droben?

Prometheus (*Autumn 1774*)

Go cover up your heaven, Zeus,
With cloudy haze!
And practise, like some boy
Topping thistle-heads,
Your strength on oaks and mountain peaks!   5
Still you must leave standing
This my earth,
And my shelter
Which you did not build,
And this my hearth   10
Whose glowing heat you envy me.

There's nothing more pitiful
Under the sun than you gods.
You feed your majesty   15
With meagre victuals
Of sacrifices
And vaporous prayer,
And would be starving were not
Children and beggars   20
Credulous simpletons.

When I was a child,
Didn't know which way to go,
My bewildered eye turned
To the sun, as if up there were   25
An ear to hear my lamentations,
A heart like mine
With mercy to comfort the afflicted.

Who helped me counter
The Titans' arrogance?   30
From death who was it rescued me,
From slavery?
Was it not you that accomplished all,
Heart in sacred glow?
And yet glowed, young and good,   35
Deluded, with gratitude
To that sleeping one up there?

Ich dich ehren? Wofür?
Hast du die Schmerzen gelindert
Je des Beladenen?   40
Hast du die Tränen gestillet
Je des Geängsteten?
Hat nicht mich zum Manne geschmiedet
Die allmächtige Zeit
Und das ewige Schicksal,   45
Meine Herrn und deine?

Wähntest du etwa,
Ich sollte das Leben hassen,
In Wüsten fliehn,
Weil nicht alle Knabenmorgen-   50
Blütenträume reiften?

Hier sitz' ich, forme Menschen
Nach meinem Bilde,
Ein Geschlecht, das mir gleich sei,
Zu leiden, weinen,   55
Genießen und zu freuen sich,
Und dein nicht zu achten,
Wie ich.

[Freudvoll und Leidvoll – aus *Egmont*]

Freudvoll
Und leidvoll,
Gedankenvoll sein,
Langen
Und bangen   5
In schwebender Pein,
Himmelhoch jauchzend,
Zum Tode betrübt;
Glücklich allein
Ist die Seele, die liebt.   10

I honour you? For what?
Did you just once ease the torments
Of him who was burdened? 40
Did you just once still the weeping
Of him who was anguished?
Was not I made a man on the anvil
Of all-powerful time
And of fate everlasting, 45
My masters and yours?

Did you imagine
Perhaps I would hate existence,
Run off to deserts,
If not all my boyhood morning's 50
Blossom-dreaming fruited?

Here I sit, fashion humans
In my own image,
A breed to be my equal,
To suffer, sorrow, 55
To enjoy and be joyful,
And to ignore you,
Like me.

[Untitled – from *Egmont*][3] (1774–5)

Glad heart
And sad heart,
And weighed down with thought,
Nearing
And fearing 5
In torment still caught,
Shouting the skies out,
Now ready to die,
Happy alone
Is the heart on love's high. 10

Neue Liebe, neues Leben

Herz, mein Herz, was soll das geben,
Was bedränget dich so sehr?
Welch ein fremdes neues Leben –
Ich erkenne dich nicht mehr.
Weg ist alles, was du liebtest,   5
Weg, worum du dich betrübtest,
Weg dein Fleiß und deine Ruh –
Ach, wie kamst du nur dazu?

Fesselt dich die Jugendblüte,
Diese liebliche Gestalt,   10
Dieser Blick voll Treu und Güte
Mit unendlicher Gewalt?
Will ich rasch mich ihr entziehen,
Mich ermannen, ihr entfliehen,
Führet mich im Augenblick –   15
Ach – mein Weg zu ihr zurück.

Und an diesem Zauberfädchen,
Das sich nicht zerreißen läßt,
Hält das liebe lose Mädchen
Mich so wider Willen fest.   20
Muß in ihrem Zauberkreise
Leben nun auf ihre Weise;
Die Verändrung, ach, wie groß!
Liebe, Liebe, laß mich los!

Lilis Park

Ist doch keine Menagerie
So bunt als meiner Lili ihre!
Sie hat darin die wunderbarsten Tiere
Und kriegt sie 'rein, weiß selbst nicht wie.
O wie sie hüpfen, laufen, trappeln,   5
Mit abgestumpften Flügeln zappeln,
Die armen Prinzen allzumal,
In nie gelöschter Liebesqual!

'Wie hieß die Fee? Lili?' – Fragt nicht nach ihr!
Kennt ihr sie nicht, so danket Gott dafür.   10

New Love, New Life (Early 1775)

Heart, my heart, what are you doing?
What's oppressing you so sore?
Strange, this new life you're pursuing –
I don't know you any more.
Gone is all you loved, all gladness,   5
Gone now all that troubling sadness,
Diligence, and rest, all gone –
Oh, what was it brought this on?

Are you gripped by youth all flowering?
By this lovely form's amaze,   10
By the endless overpowering
Of this kind and faithful gaze?
If I say that I'll not see her,
Steel myself and try to flee her,
Instantly I'm on a track –   15
Oh – that simply leads me back.

On this thread that nothing severs,
Magic spun with magic skill,
This girl, winsome-wilful, tethers
Me so much against my will: 20
In her magic circle's passions
My life now she rules and fashions.
Oh, the change, how great a blow!
Love, oh love, oh let me go!

Lili's Park (1775)

There's no other menagerie
Like my Lili's ownest!
The strangest creatures she traps all alonest
And no one knows how, not even she.
With wings clipped back o how they flutter,   5
O how they jump and run and scutter,
The poor poor princes, what a rout,
In pangs of love they can't dowse out!

'Her name, this sorceress? Lili?' – Don't ask again!
If you don't know, thank God who kept you sane.   10

Welch ein Geräusch, welch ein Gegacker,
Wenn sie sich in die Türe stellt
Und in der Hand das Futterkörbchen hält!
Welch ein Gequiek, welch ein Gequacker!
Alle Bäume, alle Büsche   15
Scheinen lebendig zu werden:
So stürzen sich ganze Herden
Zu ihren Füßen, sogar im Bassin die Fische
Patschen ungeduldig mit den Köpfen heraus;
Und sie streut dann das Futter aus   20
Mit einem Blick – Götter zu entzücken,
Geschweige die Bestien. Da geht's an ein Picken,
An ein Schlürfen, an ein Hacken;
Sie stürzen einander über die Nacken,
Schieben sich, drängen sich, reißen sich,   25
Jagen sich, ängsten sich, beißen sich,
Und das all um ein Stückchen Brot,
Das, trocken, aus den schönen Händen schmeckt,
Als hätt' es in Ambrosia gesteckt.

Aber der Blick auch, der Ton,   30
Wenn sie ruft: Pipi! Pipi!
Zöge den Adler Jupiters vom Thron;
Der Venus Taubenpaar,
Ja der eitle Pfau sogar,
Ich schwöre, sie kämen,   35
Wenn sie den Ton von weitem nur vernähmen.

Denn so hat sie aus des Waldes Nacht
Einen Bären, ungeleckt und ungezogen,
Unter ihren Beschluß hereinbetrogen,
Unter die zahme Kompanie gebracht   40
Und mit den andern zahm gemacht –
Bis auf einen gewissen Punkt, versteht sich!
Wie schön und ach! wie gut
Schien sie zu sein! Ich hätte mein Blut
Gegeben, um ihre Blumen zu begießen.   45

'Ihr sagtet: ich! Wie? Wer?'
Gut denn, ihr Herrn, grad aus: Ich bin der Bär!
In einem Filetschurz gefangen
An einem Seidenfaden ihr zu Füßen.
Doch wie das alles zugegangen,   50

O what a noise, o what a cackle,
When in the doorway at last she comes
And holds in her hands the basket of crumbs!
O all the squeals, o all the quackle!
All the trees and all the bushes   15
Seem to become animated:
Whole hordes of them agitated
Rush to her feet, and each impatient fish pushes
Its head from the bassin and splashes in and out;
And then she strews the feed about   20
With such a look – the gods befopping,
Let alone the creatures. And then starts the chopping
And the slurping and the pecking;
They're higgledy-piggledy neck and necking,
Shove themselves, crush themseves, fight themselves,   25
Chase themselves, fright themselves, bite themselves,
And all that for a crust of bread
That, bone-dry, from those lovely finger tips
Has all the taste of ambrosial sips.

But then that look, and that tone   30
When she cries: Tweetwee! Tweetwee!
Jupiter's eagle she'd pull from his throne;
And Venus' doves twain,
Even the peacock so vain,
I swear they'd come ruffled   35
If they heard that tone even far off and muffled.

Just so in the forest's night she caught
One big bear, unpolished and no breeding,
Mastered him by sheer misleading,
Him to her tame entourage she brought   40
And with the others tamed and taught –
Of course with a certain point excepted!
How lovely o! how good
She seemed to be! All of my blood
I would have given to water her flowers.   45

'But you said: I! Who? Why?'
Right then, gentlemen, straight: The bear am I!
Enmeshed in a filmy lacework therefore,
And at her feet on silky thread thus tethered.
But all about the how and wherefore   50

Erzähl' ich euch zur andern Zeit;
Dazu bin ich zu wütig heut'.

Denn ha! steh' ich so an der Ecke
Und hör' von weitem das Geschnatter,
Seh' das Geflitter, das Geflatter,   55
Kehr' ich mich um
Und brumm'
Und renne rückwärts eine Strecke
Und seh' mich um
Und brumm'   60
Und laufe wieder eine Strecke,
Und kehr' doch endlich wieder um.

Dann fängt's auf einmal an zu rasen,
Ein mächt'ger Geist schnaubt aus der Nasen,
Es wildzt die innere Natur.   65
Was, du ein Tor, ein Häschen nur!
So ein Pipi! Eichhörnchen, Nuß zu knacken!
Ich sträube meinen borst'gen Nacken,
Zu dienen ungewöhnt.
Ein jedes aufgestutzte Bäumchen höhnt   70
Mich an! ich flieh' vom Boulingreen,
Vom niedlich glatt gemähten Grase.
Der Buchsbaum zieht mir eine Nase!
Ich flieh' ins dunkelste Gebüsche hin,
Durchs Gehäge zu dringen,   75
Über die Planken zu springen.
Mir versagt Klettern und Sprung,
Ein Zauber bleit mich nieder,
Ein Zauber häkelt mich wieder,
Ich arbeite mich ab, und bin ich matt genung,   80
Dann lieg' ich an gekünstelten Kaskaden
Und kau' und wein' und wälze halb mich tot,
Und ach! es hören meine Not
Nur porzellanene Oreaden.

Auf einmal! ach, es dringt   85
Ein seliges Gefühl durch alle meine Glieder:
Sie ist's, die dort in ihrer Laube singt!
Ich hör' die liebe, liebe Stimme wieder,
Die ganze Luft ist warm, ist blütevoll.
Ach! singt sie wohl, daß ich sie hören soll?   90

I'll tell you at some other stage;
Today I'm in too big a rage.

For oh! in one of my corner places
I stand and hear the distant natter,
See the far off flitter-flatter, 55
Turn round and scowl
And growl
And run off backwards just a few paces
And look round and scowl
And growl 60
And run again a few more paces
And yet at last I return to the fowl.

Then suddenly mad rage is starting,
A mighty spirit snorts nose-smarting,
Now wilds in me the inner bear. 65
What, you a fool, a simple hare!
Such a Tweetwee! A nut-cracking squirrel that idles!
My bristly neck rears up and bridles,
Unwonted service shocks.
And every little well-trained tree looks and mocks 70
At me! I rush from the bouling green,
From those sleek lawns that irritate me.
The box-tree cocks a snook to bait me!
I seek dark undergrowth, seek not to be seen,
Try to break through the hedges 75
And jump the fence round the edges.
But climbing and jumping all misfire,
A leaden spell now strikes me,
A spell that hooks and spikes me,
I writhe and toil, and then when I tire 80
I lie in cascading fountain jets
And gnash and wail till I'm nearly gone
But oh! my torment's heard by none
Save porcelain Oread statuettes.

Suddenly! oh, a sheer 85
Sense of bliss pierces every limb and member:
It's she who sings in the arbour here,
I hear that dear, dear voice that I remember,
The air is all warm, a flowering ecstasy,
Oh, perhaps her song is meant for me? 90

Ich dringe zu, tret' alle Sträuche nieder,
Die Büsche fliehn, die Bäume weichen mir,
Und so – zu ihren Füßen liegt das Tier.

Sie sieht es an: 'Ein Ungeheuer! doch drollig!
Für einen Bären zu mild,   95
Für einen Pudel zu wild;
So zottig, täpsig, knollig!'
Sie streicht ihm mit dem Füßchen übern Rücken;
Er denkt im Paradiese zu sein.
Wie ihn alle sieben Sinne jücken!   100
Und sie – sieht ganz gelassen drein.
Ich küss' ihre Schuhe, kau' an den Sohlen,
So sittig, als ein Bär nur mag;
Ganz sachte heb' ich mich und schmiege mich verstohlen
Leis an ihr Knie – am günst'gen Tag   105
Läßt sie's geschehn und kraut mir um die Ohren
Und patscht mich mit mutwillig derbem Schlag –
Ich knurr', in Wonne neu geboren.
Dann fordert sie mit süßem, eitlem Spotte:
'Allons tout doux! eh la menotte!   110
Et faites Serviteur,
Comme un joli Seigneur.'
So treibt sie's fort mit Spiel und Lachen!
Es hofft der oft betrogne Tor;
Doch will er sich ein bißchen unnütz machen,   115
Hält sie ihn kurz als wie zuvor.

Doch hat sie auch ein Fläschchen Balsam-Feuers,
Dem keiner Erde Honig gleicht,
Wovon sie wohl einmal, von Lieb und Treu erweicht,
Um die verlechzten Lippen ihres Ungeheuers   120
Ein Tröpfchen mit der Fingerspitze streicht
Und wieder flieht und mich mir überläßt,
Und ich dann, losgebunden, fest
Gebannt bin, immer nach ihr ziehe,
Sie suche, schaudre, wieder fliehe –   125
So läßt sie den zerstörten Armen gehn,
Ist seiner Lust, ist seinen Schmerzen still;
Ha, manchmal läßt sie mir die Tür halb offen stehn,
Seitblickt mich spottend an, ob ich nicht fliehen will.

I press towards it, trampling shrubs I meet,
The bushes rush away, the trees retreat,
And so – again the creature lies at her feet.

She looks at it: 'A monster! but waggy!
For a bear too mild,   95
For a poodle too wild:
So shambly, knobbly, shaggy!'
His back with her neat little foot she tickles;
He thinks that he's in Paradise.
How each of his seven senses prickles!   100
And she – looks on with clear calm eyes.
I kiss her shoes, I chew the soles shyly,
Quite decently really for only a bear;
Cautiously I rise and snuggle inching slyly
Up to her knee – if the day's set fair   105
She lets it happen and scratches my furry
Ears and heftily pats my hair –
New-born in bliss I growl all purry.
Then her sweet empty mockery puts me on the spot:
'*Allons tout doux! eh la menotte!*   110
Et faites Serviteur,
Comme un joli Seigneur.'
So she carries on in play and laughter!
The oft duped dope has hope once more
But if he gets a little forward after   115
She keeps him short just like before.

But she's also got a balsam-fire,
Unlike this earth's honey, just a little phial,
And sometimes when she's softened by love and loyalty a while
On the parched lips of her monster about to expire   120
Her finger strokes a droplet to reconcile,
And again she's off and leaves me to stew;
And I, liberated, am anew
Enspelled, am pulled to see her,
I seek her, shudder, again I flee her –   125
Thus she treats this wretch destroyed so sore,
If he's happy, or hurt, no word from her;
O yes, often she does half-open the door,
Glances mocking to see if escape's what I prefer.

Und ich! – Götter, ist's in euren Händen,   130
Dieses dumpfe Zauberwerk zu enden:
Wie dank' ich, wenn ihr mir die Freiheit schafft!
Doch sendet ihr mir keine Hilfe nieder –
Nicht ganz umsonst reck' ich so meine Glieder:
Ich fühl's! ich schwör's! Noch hab' ich Kraft.   135

Auf dem See

(Spätere Fassung)

Und frische Nahrung, neues Blut
Saug' ich aus freier Welt;
Wie ist Natur so hold und gut,
Die mich am Busen hält!
Die Welle wieget unsern Kahn   5
Im Rudertakt hinauf,
Und Berge, wolkig himmelan,
Begegnen unserm Lauf.

Aug', mein Aug', was sinkst du nieder?
Goldne Träume, kommt ihr wieder?   10
Weg, du Traum, so gold du bist:
Hier auch Lieb' und Leben ist.

Auf der Welle blinken
Tausend schwebende Sterne,
Weiche Nebel trinken   15
Rings die türmende Ferne;
Morgenwind umflügelt
Die beschattete Bucht,
Und im See bespiegelt
Sich die reifende Frucht.   20

Herbstgefühl

Fetter grüne, du Laub,
Am Rebengeländer,
Hier mein Fenster herauf.
Gedrängter quellet,
Zwillingsbeeren, und reifet   5

And I! – Ye gods, if you have power to sunder   130
This stupefying magic spell I'm under
How I'll thank you if you set me free!
But if you won't help me now in good season –
Don't think I stretch these limbs without a reason:
I feel it! I swear it! I've still got strength in me.   135

On the Lake *(June 1775)*

(Later Version)

And now I suck fresh food, new blood,
From all the world with zest;
Dear nature, how she's fair and good
Who holds me to her breast!
The rocking wave lifts up our boat   5
In rhythm of the oars,
And mountains cloudy skywards float
To cut across our course.

Eyes, my eyes, why are you closing?
Golden dreams, once more proposing?   10
Dream, begone, though gold you be:
Here too love and life I see.

Stars in thousands blinking
Float on waves passing by,
Downy mists are drinking   15
Distance towering high:
Morning wind wings gently
Round the shadow-filled bay,
Ripening fruit contently
Mirrors itself in the sway.   20

Autumn Feeling *(Autumn 1775)*

Green more juicy, you leaves,
On vines of this trellis,
Up to my window here.
And swell more compact,
Twin-grown berries, and ripen   5

Schneller und glänzend voller.
Euch brütet der Mutter Sonne
Scheideblick, euch umsäuselt
Des holden Himmels
Fruchtende Fülle.   10
Euch kühlet des Mondes
Freundlicher Zauberhauch,
Und euch betauen, ach,
Aus diesen Augen
Der ewig belebenden Liebe   15
Vollschwellende Tränen.

Warum gabst du uns die tiefen Blicke

Warum gabst du uns die tiefen Blicke,
Unsre Zukunft ahndungsvoll zu schaun,
Unsrer Liebe, unserm Erdenglücke
Wähnend selig nimmer hinzutraun?
Warum gabst uns, Schicksal, die Gefühle,   5
Uns einander in das Herz zu sehn
Um durch all' die seltenen Gewühle
Unser wahr Verhältnis auszuspähn?

Ach, so viele tausend Menschen kennen,
Dumpf sich treibend, kaum ihr eigen Herz,   10
Schweben zwecklos hin und her und rennen
Hoffnungslos in unversehnem Schmerz;
Jauchzen wieder, wenn der schnellen Freuden
Unerwart'te Morgenröte tagt.
Nur uns armen liebevollen beiden   15
Ist das wechselseit'ge Glück versagt,
Uns zu lieben, ohn' uns zu verstehen,
In dem andern sehn, was er nie war,
Immer frisch auf Traumglück auszugehen
Und zu schwanken auch in Traumgefahr.   20

Glücklich, den ein leerer Traum beschäftigt!
Glücklich, dem die Ahndung eitel wär'!
Jede Gegenwart und jeder Blick bekräftigt
Traum und Ahndung leider uns noch mehr.
Sag', was will das Schicksal uns bereiten?   25

Quicker and gleaming fuller.
You brood of the sun's maternal
Afterglance, you are fanned by
The gracious heaven's
Fertile abundance.   10
You're cooled by the moon's
Friendly enspelling breath,
And you are dewed, alas,
From out these eyes by
The ever enlivening love in   15
Tears swelling to fullness.

Why give us deep vision ... ? (April 1776)

Why give us deep vision so far-sighted
That foreboding we our future see,
That by love and earthly joys delighted
We cannot in bliss deluded be?
Why for us, fate, did you by this feeling   5
Bring our hearts into each other's scope,
So our true relationship revealing
As through explorations strange we grope?

Oh, so many thousand men drift feckless,
Sluggish-sensed, and hardly know their hearts,   10
Hover purposeless and then rush reckless
Through the pain of hopeless fits and starts;
Shout for joy again when darting pleasure
Unexpected dawns all rosy-eyed.
Just to us poor lovers is the treasure   15
Of that mutual happiness denied:
As we never were, to see each other,
Each to love yet not the other know,
Chase the happiness our dreams discover
And in peril-dreams sway to and fro.   20

Bliss, absorbed in empty dream's romances!
Bliss, foreboding brushed aside as wrong!
Sadly all the present, all our glances,
Make foreboding and our dream more strong.
Tell me, what is fate for us preparing?   25

Sag', wie band es uns so rein genau?
Ach, du warst in abgelebten Zeiten
Meine Schwester oder meine Frau;

Kanntest jeden Zug in meinem Wesen,
Spähtest, wie die reinste Nerve klingt,   30
Konntest mich mit einem Blicke lesen,
Den so schwer ein sterblich Aug' durchdringt.
Tropftest Mäßigung dem heißen Blute,
Richtetest den wilden irren Lauf,
Und in deinen Engelsarmen ruhte   35
Die zerstörte Brust sich wieder auf;
Hieltest zauberleicht ihn angebunden
Und vergaukeltest ihm manchen Tag.
Welche Seligkeit glich jenen Wonnestunden,
Da er dankbar dir zu Füßen lag,   40
Fühlt' sein Herz an deinem Herzen schwellen,
Fühlte sich in deinem Auge gut,
Alle seine Sinnen sich erhellen
Und beruhigen sein brausend Blut.

Und von allem dem schwebt ein Erinnern   45
Nur noch um das ungewisse Herz,
Fühlt die alte Wahrheit ewig gleich im Innern,
Und der neue Zustand wird ihm Schmerz.
Und wir scheinen uns nur halb beseelet,
Dämmernd ist um uns der hellste Tag.   50
Glücklich, daß das Schicksal, das uns quälet,
Uns doch nicht verändern mag.

Rastlose Liebe

Dem Schnee, dem Regen,
Dem Wind entgegen,
Im Dampf der Klüfte,
Durch Nebeldüfte,
Immer zu! Immer zu!   5
Ohne Rast und Ruh!

Lieber durch Leiden
Möcht' ich mich schlagen,
Als so viel Freuden

Tell me, how it made us fit so true?
Oh, in some past life that we were sharing
You as sister or my wife I knew;

You knew every aspect of my being,
Noted how my very nerves vibrate,   30
Read me with one single glance far-seeing,
Me whom mortal eyes can't penetrate.
You dosed fevered blood with moderation,
Rectified the errant course run wild,
And the ravaged heart found restoration,   35
In your angel arms was reconciled;
Held him lightly bound in magic tether
Conjuring away the idling day.
Where's the bliss to match those hours together
When so grateful at your feet he lay,   40
Felt against your heart his heart grow lighter,
Saw himself in your eyes and felt good,
All his senses quickening and brighter
And a calming in his seething blood.

And from all of that alone the faltering   45
Memories round the unsure heart remain
While the former truth within still stays unaltering,
And its new condition turns to pain.
We feel we are only half existing,
Twilight dims for us the brightest day.   50
Glad that fate on torment is insisting
Yet won't alter us in any way.

Love without Peace (May 1776)

'Gainst snow, 'gainst raining,
'Gainst head wind straining,
In chasms seething,
Through haze-mists wreathing,
Always on! always on!   5
No rest, peace all gone!

Better be sharing
Suffering and sadness
Rather than bearing

Des Lebens ertragen.   10
Alle das Neigen
Von Herzen zu Herzen,
Ach wie so eigen
Schaffet das Schmerzen!

Wie soll ich fliehen?   15
Wälderwärts ziehen?
Alles vergebens!
Krone des Lebens,
Glück ohne Ruh,
Liebe, bist du!   20

An den Geist des Johannes Secundus

Lieber, heiliger, großer Küsser,
Der du mir's in lechzend atmender
Glückseligkeit fast vorgetan hast!
Wem soll ich's klagen, klagt' ich dir's nicht!
Dir, dessen Lieder wie ein warmes Kissen   5
Heilender Kräuter mir unters Herz sich legten,
Daß es wieder aus dem krampfigen Starren
Erdetreibens klopfend sich erholte.
Ach, wie klag' ich dir's, daß meine Lippe blutet,
Mir gespalten ist und erbärmlich schmerzet,   10
Meine Lippe, die so viel gewohnt ist
Von der Liebe süßem Glück zu schwellen
Und, wie eine goldne Himmelspforte,
Lallende Seligkeit aus- und einzustammeln.
Gesprungen ist sie! Nicht vom Biß der Holden,   15
Die, in voller ringsumfangender Liebe,
Mehr möcht' haben von mir, und möchte mich Ganzen
Ganz erküssen, und fressen, und was sie könnte!
Nicht gesprungen, weil nach ihrem Hauche
Meine Lippen unheilige Lüfte entweihten.   20
Ach, gesprungen, weil mich, öden, kalten,
Über beizenden Reif der Herbstwind anpackt.
Und da ist Traubensaft und der Saft der Bienen,
An meines Herdes treuem Feuer vereinigt,
Der soll mir helfen! Wahrlich, er hilft nicht: 25
Denn von der Liebe alles heilendem
Gift-Balsam ist kein Tröpfchen drunter.

A life of such gladness.   10
All that attraction
Of heart to heart tending,
Strange, how its action
Makes pain unending!

How to get free now?   15
Forestwards flee now?
Vain, all such scheming!
Life's crown all gleaming,
Restlessness too,
Love, that is you!   20

To the Spirit of Johannes Secundus[4] (November 1776)

Kind, and holy, famed for kisses,
You who so nearly pre-charted me
In my breathing thirsting ecstasy!
To whom should I lament if not to you!
You, whose poems were a heart's-ease to me,   5
Supporting me like a warming pillow of healing herbs,
So that once again from these earthly spasms
My heart recovered to beat once more.
Oh, how to tell you that my lip is bleeding,
That it's split and hurts so pitiable painful,   10
This lip of mine that is so accustomed
To swell with love's sweet happiness
And, like a golden portal of heaven,
To take in and give out the tones of blissful delirium.
Yes, it is split! Not from the bite of my fair one   15
Who, in the all-embracing fullness of her loving,
Wants only more of me, and wants the whole of me
Entirely in her kisses, devouring, whatever she could!
Not split because my lips were desecrated
By profane airs after she had breathed on me.   20
Split, alas, because I, cold, desolate,
Was seized by autumn winds in the cutting frost.
And now there's the juice of grapes and the honey-bee's juices,
Both together by my friendly fire on the hearth,
That's there to help me! In fact, it doesn't help: 25
For of love's healing poisonous balm
They've not got a single droplet between them.

Liebebedürfnis

(Spätere Fassung des vorigen)

Wer vernimmt mich? ach, wem soll ich's klagen?
Wer's vernähme, würd' er mich bedauern?
Ach! die Lippe, die so manche Freude
Sonst genossen hat und sonst gegeben,
Ist gespalten, und sie schmerzt erbärmlich.   5
Und sie ist nicht etwa wund geworden,
Weil die Liebste mich zu wild ergriffen,
Hold mich angebissen, daß sie fester
Sich des Freunds versichernd ihn genösse:
Nein, das zarte Lippchen ist gesprungen,   10
Weil nun über Reif und Frost die Winde
Spitz und scharf und lieblos mir begegnen.

Und nun soll mir Saft der edlen Traube,
Mit dem Saft der Bienen bei dem Feuer
Meines Herds vereinigt, Lindrung schaffen.   15
Ach, was will das helfen, mischt die Liebe
Nicht ein Tröpfchen ihres Balsams drunter?

Harzreise im Winter

Dem Geier gleich,
Der auf schweren Morgenwolken
Mit sanftem Fittich ruhend
Nach Beute schaut,
Schwebe mein Lied.   5

Denn ein Gott hat
Jedem seine Bahn
Vorgezeichnet,
Die der Glückliche
Rasch zum freudigen   10
Ziele rennt;
Wem aber Unglück
Das Herz zusammenzog,
Er sträubt vergebens
Sich gegen die Schranken   15
Des ehernen Fadens,
Den die doch bittre Schere
Nur einmal löst.

Need for Love

(Later version of the preceding poem, between 1776 and 1789)

Who will hear me? oh, to whom lament it?
He who heard it, would he feel my suffering?
Oh, this lip which knew so many moments
Taking pleasures as well as giving pleasures,
Has been split, and miserably it hurts me.   5
Don't imagine that its chafe and soreness
Came because my dear was too voracious,
Bit me as she graced me, wanting only
More securely to enjoy her lover:
No, this delicate lip is split and tender   10
Just because the winds and frost confront me
Joined in sharp and spiteful combination.

And now it seems that the vine as juice ennobled
With the juice of bees, together at my fireside,
Are joined to comfort me and give me easement.   15
Oh, what use is that unless love mixes
One single droplet of its soothing lotion?

Winter Journey in the Harz *(December 1777)*

To match the hawk,
Who on heavy clouds of morning
At rest with languid pinion
Seeks out his prize,
Soar now my song.   5

For a god has
Set for each his course
Predetermined
Which the fortunate
Swiftly runs to its   10
Joyful term;
But if misfortune
Has garrotted his heart
He chafes in vain at
The fatal thread's limit   15
That tethers like iron,
Loosed by shearing that's bitter
And only once.

In Dickichtsschauer
Drängt sich das rauhe Wild,　　　　　　　20
Und mit den Sperlingen
Haben längst die Reichen
In ihre Sümpfe sich gesenkt.

Leicht ist's, folgen dem Wagen,
Den Fortuna führt,　　　　　　　25
Wie der gemächliche Troß
Auf gebesserten Wegen
Hinter des Fürsten Einzug.

Aber abseits, wer ist's?
Ins Gebüsch verliert sich sein Pfad,　　　　　　　30
Hinter ihm schlagen
Die Sträuche zusammen,
Das Gras steht wieder auf,
Die Öde verschlingt ihn.

Ach, wer heilet die Schmerzen　　　　　　　35
Des, dem Balsam zu Gift ward?
Der sich Menschenhaß
Aus der Fülle der Liebe trank.
Erst verachtet, nun ein Verächter,
Zehrt er heimlich auf　　　　　　　40
Seinen eignen Wert
In ungnügender Selbstsucht.

Ist auf deinem Psalter,
Vater der Liebe, ein Ton
Seinem Ohre vernehmlich,　　　　　　　45
So erquicke sein Herz!
Öffne den umwölkten Blick
Über die tausend Quellen
Neben dem Durstenden
In der Wüste!　　　　　　　50

Der du der Freuden viel schaffst,
Jedem ein überfließend Maß,
Segne die Brüder der Jagd
Auf der Fährte des Wilds
Mit jugendlichem Übermut　　　　　　　55
Fröhlicher Mordsucht,
Späte Rächer des Unbills,

To fearsome thickets
Fierce wild beasts repair,   20
And with the reed sparrows
Rich men have long since wandered
Off to their winter hide in swamps.

Easy, following the chariot
When Dame Fortune steers,   25
Just like the footfollower's ease
When the prince makes his entry
Over the road's new surface.

Over there though, who's that?
See, his path is lost in the scrub,   30
Hard on his footsteps
The bushes are closing,
The grass springs back again,
The wasteland devours him.

Oh, who will heal the tormented,   35
Him whose balm turned to poison
Drinking misanthropy
From the copious wells of love?
First despised, and now too a despiser,
He consumes unseen   40
His own value's core
In self-seeking that sates not.

If your psalter's compass,
All-loving Father, has tones
Which can open his hearing   45
Let them freshen his heart!
Open up his clouded eye
To see the thousand wellsprings
Close by him thirsting there in the desert!

You who have made joys in plenty,   50
To each an overflowing measure,
Bless now the friends of the hunt
On the trail of the beast
In spirited excess of youth's
Murderous gaiety,   55
Late avengers of evils

Dem schon Jahre vergeblich
Wehrt mit Knütteln der Bauer.

Aber den Einsamen hüll'   60
In deine Goldwolken,
Umgib mit Wintergrün,
Bis die Rose wieder heranreift,
Die feuchten Haare,
O Liebe, deines Dichters!   65

Mit der dämmernden Fackel
Leuchtest du ihm
Durch die Furten bei Nacht,
Über grundlose Wege
Auf öden Gefilden,   70
Mit dem tausendfarbigen Morgen
Lachst du ins Herz ihm;
Mit dem beizenden Sturm
Trägst du ihn hoch empor.
Winterströme stürzen vom Felsen   75
In seine Psalmen,
Und Altar des lieblichsten Danks
Wird ihm des gefürchteten Gipfels
Schneebehangner Scheitel,
Den mit Geisterreihen   80
Kränzten ahnende Völker.

Du stehst mit unerforschtem Busen
Geheimnisvoll-offenbar
Über der erstaunten Welt
Und schaust aus Wolken   85
Auf ihre Reiche und Herrlichkeit,
Die du aus den Adern deiner Brüder
Neben dir wässerst.

Sag' ich's euch, geliebte Bäume

Sag' ich's euch, geliebte Bäume,
Die ich ahndevoll gepflanzt,
Als die wunderbarsten Träume
Morgenrötlich mich umtanzt?
Ach, ihr wißt es, wie ich liebe,   5

Which the peasant for ages
Vainly resists with bludgeons.

But to the lonely one bring
Your golden cloudwrapping, 60
Bind round with evergreen
Till the rose once again matures
The winter-drenched hair,
Oh Love, of your poet!

With your glimmering lantern 65
You light his way
Through the fords in the night,
Over treacherous footpaths
On barren terrain;
With your thousand colours of morning 70
Your laughter is in his heart;
With the acid-sharp storm
High you transport him aloft.
Winter torrents plunge from the cliff tops
To flood his anthems, 75
For an altar of grateful love
He looks to the much-dreaded summit's
Snow-enveloped very top
Which the awe of nations
Wreathed with gathering spirits. 80

You stand with breast impenetrable
Mysterious and evident
Over the astonished world
And look from clouds
On all its kingdoms and its glory 85
Still nourished by you from the veins of brothers
Standing beside you.

Darling trees, do you need telling (1780)

Darling trees, do you need telling,
You I planted, half aware,
When those dawn-red dreams enspelling
Danced so wondrous in the air?
How I love, oh, you know surely, 5

Die so schön mich wiederliebt,
Die den reinsten meiner Triebe
Mir noch reiner wiedergibt.

Wachset wie aus meinem Herzen,
Treibet in die Luft hinein; 10
Denn ich grub viel Freud und Schmerzen
Unter eure Wurzeln ein.
Bringet Schatten, traget Früchte,
Neue Freude jeden Tag:
Nur daß ich sie dichte, dichte, 15
Dicht bei ihr genießen mag!

Das Göttliche

Edel sei der Mensch,
Hilfreich und gut!
Denn das allein
Unterscheidet ihn
Von allen Wesen, 5
Die wir kennen.

Heil den unbekannten
Höhern Wesen,
Die wir ahnen!
Ihnen gleiche der Mensch! 10
Sein Beispiel lehr' uns
Jene glauben.

Denn unfühlend
Ist die Natur:
Es leuchtet die Sonne 15
Über Bös' und Gute,
Und dem Verbrecher
Glänzen wie dem Besten
Der Mond und die Sterne.

Wind und Ströme, 20
Donner und Hagel
Rauschen ihren Weg
Und ergreifen
Vorübereilend
Einen um den andern. 25

Her who loves me answeringly
And who gives me back more purely
That most pure of drives in me.

From my heart, then, grow and flourish,
Thrust up striving in the air;   10
For your roots have soils that nourish,
Joy and pains I buried there.
Give me shade, give fruit's rich blessing,
Every day new joys confer:
Give, but let me then be pressing,   15
Pressing, pressing close to her!

The Divine (1783)

Noble, let man be,
Helpful and good!
For that alone
Distinguishes him
From all beings   5
That we know of.

Hail to the unknown
Higher beings
Sensed in the mind!
Let man be as they are!   10
His example teach us
Belief in them.

For nature
Is unfeeling:
The sun's light shines   15
On the wicked and the good,
And transgressor and the best
Alike see the gleaming
Of the moon and the stars.

Wind and waters,   20
Thunder and hailstones
Roar on their course
And hurrying on
Seize as they go
One after the other.   25

Auch so das Glück
Tappt unter die Menge,
Faßt bald des Knaben
Lockige Unschuld,
Bald auch den kahlen   30
Schuldigen Scheitel.

Nach ewigen, ehrnen,
Großen Gesetzen
Müssen wir alle
Unseres Daseins   35
Kreise vollenden.

Nur allein der Mensch
Vermag das Unmögliche:
Er unterscheidet,
Wählet und richtet;   40
Er kann dem Augenblick
Dauer verleihen.

Er allein darf
Den Guten lohnen,
Den Bösen strafen,   45
Heilen und retten,
Alles Irrende, Schweifende
Nützlich verbinden.

Und wir verehren
Die Unsterblichen,   50
Als wären sie Menschen,
Täten im großen,
Was der Beste im kleinen
Tut oder möchte.

Der edle Mensch   55
Sei hilfreich und gut!
Unermüdet schaff' er
Das Nützliche, Rechte,
Sei uns ein Vorbild
Jener geahneten Wesen!   60

So too fortune
Gropes among the crowd,
Grasping now the child's
Curly-haired innocence
Now too the balding   30
Head of the guilty.

By eternal, iron,
Mighty laws
Must each and all of us
Complete the circles   35
Of our existence.

Only man alone
Can do the impossible:
He can distinguish,
Chooses and judges;   40
He can endow
The moment with permanence.

He alone may
Reward the good man,
Punish the wicked,   45
Restore and rescue,
Usefully bind
All that errs and wanders.

And we venerate
The immortal ones,   50
As if they were humans,
And did on the grand scale
What the best in his small way
Does or would wish to.

Let the noble man   55
Be helpful and good!
Untiring let him do
The right and the useful,
And pre-figure for us
Those sensed higher beings.   60

Zueignung

Der Morgen kam; es scheuchten seine Tritte
Den leisen Schlaf, der mich gelind umfing,
Daß ich, erwacht, aus meiner stillen Hütte
Den Berg hinauf mit frischer Seele ging;
Ich freute mich bei einem jeden Schritte   5
Der neuen Blume, die voll Tropfen hing;
Der junge Tag erhob sich mit Entzücken,
Und alles war erquickt, mich zu erquicken.

Und wie ich stieg, zog von dem Fluß der Wiesen
Ein Nebel sich in Streifen sacht hervor,   10
Er wich und wechselte, mich zu umfließen,
Und wuchs geflügelt mir ums Haupt empor.
Des schönen Blicks sollt' ich nicht mehr genießen,
Die Gegend deckte mir ein trüber Flor;
Bald sah ich mich von Wolken wie umgossen   15
Und mit mir selbst in Dämmrung eingeschlossen.

Auf einmal schien die Sonne durchzudringen,
Im Nebel ließ sich eine Klarheit sehn.
Hier sank er, leise sich hinabzuschwingen,
Hier teilt' er steigend sich um Wald und Höhn.   20
Wie hofft' ich ihr den ersten Gruß zu bringen!
Sie hofft' ich nach der Trübe doppelt schön.
Der luft'ge Kampf war lange nicht vollendet,
Ein Glanz umgab mich, und ich stand geblendet.

Bald machte mich, die Augen aufzuschlagen,   25
Ein innrer Trieb des Herzens wieder kühn,
Ich konnt' es nur mit schnellen Blicken wagen,
Denn alles schien zu brennen und zu glühn.
Da schwebte, mit den Wolken hergetragen,
Ein göttlich Weib vor meinen Augen hin,   30
Kein schöner Bild sah ich in meinem Leben,
Sie sah mich an und blieb verweilend schweben.

'Kennst du mich nicht?' sprach sie mit einem Munde,
Dem aller Lieb' und Treue Ton entfloß,
'Erkennst du mich, die ich in manche Wunde   35
Des Lebens dir den reinsten Balsam goß?
Du kennst mich wohl, an die, zu ew'gem Bunde,
Dein strebend Herz sich fest und fester schloß.

Dedication (*August 1784*)

The morning came; it drove off sleep that held me
So tenderly in slumber as I lay
And wakening me, with soul refreshed, compelled me
To leave my hut and climb the mountain way;
At every step each new-sprung flower enspelled me   5
With joy to see its dew-filled sparkling play;
The young enraptured day rose up before me,
All quickened fresh to quicken and restore me.

And as I climbed there softly crept beside me,
In swathes from meadow stream, a mist close by,   10
Receding, changing, flowing round to hide me
And soaring overhead to fill the sky.
The lovely view's refreshment was denied me,
A sombre drape the prospect for my eye;
A sea of clouds around me undulated   15
And closed in twilight I stood isolated.

The sun seemed suddenly to be defeating
The mist and there appeared a clarity.
The mist here sank, in gentle fall retreating,
Or split round woods and peaks and rose up free.   20
O how I hoped to give that light my greeting!
After gloom, I hoped, twice lovelier it must be.
The aerial strife was nowhere near decision,
Then a radiance ringed me, blinding all my vision.

But soon my eyes were opening and clearing,   25
Some drive within my heart my spirit raised,
I only dared quick glances in that searing
Where seemingly all glowed and burned and blazed.
I saw a hovering cloud-borne image nearing
And on a woman's form divine I gazed,   30
In all my life I saw no form more lovely,
She looked at me and swayed a while above me.

'Don't you know me?' from lips the words were spoken
Whence flowed all love and loyalty's dear sound,
'Know me, who when life's wounding left you broken   35
For you so often purest balm have found?
You know me well, to whom your heart in token
Of union everlastingly was bound.

Sah ich dich nicht mit heißen Herzenstränen
Als Knabe schon nach mir dich eifrig sehnen?'   40

'Ja!' rief ich aus, indem ich selig nieder
Zur Erde sank, 'lang' hab' ich dich gefühlt:
Du gabst mir Ruh, wenn durch die jungen Glieder
Die Leidenschaft sich rastlos durchgewühlt;
Du hast mir wie mit himmlischem Gefieder   45
Am heißen Tag die Stirne sanft gekühlt;
Du schenktest mir der Erde beste Gaben,
Und jedes Glück will ich durch dich nur haben!

Dich nenn' ich nicht. Zwar hör' ich dich von vielen
Gar oft genannt, und jeder heißt dich sein,   50
Ein jedes Auge glaubt auf dich zu zielen,
Fast jedem Auge wird dein Strahl zur Pein.
Ach, da ich irrte, hatt' ich viel Gespielen,
Da ich dich kenne, bin ich fast allein;
Ich muß mein Glück nur mit mir selbst genießen,   55
Dein holdes Licht verdecken und verschließen.'

Sie lächelte, sie sprach: 'Du siehst, wie klug,
Wie nötig war's, euch wenig zu enthüllen!
Kaum bist du sicher vor dem gröbsten Trug,
Kaum bist du Herr vom ersten Kinderwillen,   60
So glaubst du dich schon Übermensch genug,
Versäumst die Pflicht des Mannes zu erfüllen!
Wie viel bist du von andern unterschieden?
Erkenne dich, leb' mit der Welt in Frieden!'

'Verzeih mir', rief ich aus, 'ich meint' es gut.   65
Soll ich umsonst die Augen offen haben?
Ein froher Wille lebt in meinem Blut,
Ich kenne ganz den Wert von deinen Gaben.
Für andre wächst in mir das edle Gut,
Ich kann und will das Pfund nicht mehr vergraben!   70
Warum sucht' ich den Weg so sehnsuchtsvoll,
Wenn ich ihn nicht den Brüdern zeigen soll?'

Und wie ich sprach, sah mich das hohe Wesen
Mit einem Blick mitleid'ger Nachsicht an;
Ich konnte mich in ihrem Auge lesen,   75
Was ich verfehlt und was ich recht getan.
Sie lächelte, da war ich schon genesen,

Did I not see you with your heart's tears burning
For me already in your boyhood yearning?'   40

'Yes!' I cried out, immediately kneeling
In whelming bliss, 'it's you I long have sensed:
You gave me peace, to my young limbs brought healing
When restless passion tossed and turned and tensed;
On my hot brow you laid a cooling feeling   45
As if by gentle heavenly plumes dispensed:
You gave me gifts the best of earthly treasure,
Through you alone I'll seek all joy and pleasure!

I name you not. By others less reflective
I hear you named, each claims you as his own,   50
Though every eye thinks you are its objective
To nearly all your light strikes pain unknown.
Ah, when I erred I had friends with like perspective,
Now that I know you I am near alone;
My joy must stay a lonely contemplation   55
With your fair light locked up in isolation.'

She smiled, then spoke: 'How needful, now you see,
How wise, to refrain from self-revelations!
Scarcely from crass delusion are you free,
Scarcely you've mastered childish inclinations,   60
You claim a superhuman's quality
And so neglect all manly obligations!
Are you so special, so to be lamented?
Now know yourself, live with the world contented!'

'Forgive', I cried, 'you know it was well-meant.   65
Shall I see aimlessly when you are guiding?
My blood runs quick with good and glad intent,
Your gifts I value for their worth abiding.
For others shall my nobler wealth be spent,
My talents cannot, shall not, stay in hiding!   70
Why did I yearn to find the way to go
If not to brothers afterwards to show?'

And as I spoke the look from that high being
Was solace and indulgence for my plight;
And in her eye myself entirely seeing   75
I knew where I had failed and where done right.
She smiled, I sensed the healing and the freeing,

Zu neuen Freuden stieg mein Geist heran;
Ich konnte nun mit innigem Vertrauen
Mich zu ihr nahn und ihre Nähe schauen.   80

Da reckte sie die Hand aus in die Streifen
Der leichten Wolken und des Dufts umher;
Wie sie ihn faßte, ließ er sich ergreifen,
Er ließ sich ziehn, es war kein Nebel mehr.
Mein Auge konnt' im Tale wieder schweifen,   85
Gen Himmel blickt' ich, er war hell und hehr.
Nur sah ich sie den reinsten Schleier halten,
Er floß um sie und schwoll in tausend Falten.

'Ich kenne dich, ich kenne deine Schwächen,
Ich weiß, was Gutes in dir lebt und glimmt!'   90
So sagte sie, ich hör' sie ewig sprechen,
'Empfange hier, was ich dir lang' bestimmt!
Dem Glücklichen kann es an nichts gebrechen,
Der dies Geschenk mit stiller Seele nimmt:
Aus Morgenduft gewebt und Sonnenklarheit,   95
Der Dichtung Schleier aus der Hand der Wahrheit.

Und wenn es dir und deinen Freunden schwüle
Am Mittag wird, so wirf ihn in die Luft!
Sogleich umsäuselt Abendwindes Kühle,
Umhaucht euch Blumen-Würzgeruch und Duft.   100
Es schweigt das Wehen banger Erdgefühle,
Zum Wolkenbette wandelt sich die Gruft,
Besänftiget wird jede Lebenswelle,
Der Tag wird lieblich, und die Nacht wird helle.'

So kommt denn, Freunde, wenn auf euren Wegen   105
Des Lebens Bürde schwer und schwerer drückt,
Wenn eure Bahn ein frischerneuter Segen
Mit Blumen ziert, mit goldnen Früchten schmückt,
Wir gehn vereint dem nächsten Tag entgegen!
So leben wir, so wandeln wir beglückt.   110
Und dann auch soll, wenn Enkel um uns trauern,
Zu ihrer Lust noch unsre Liebe dauern.

My spirit rose to heights of new delight;
I neared her with deep trust and dedication,
From close nearby absorbed in contemplation.   80

And then she followed with her hand the swaying
Swathes of cloud that drifted here and there;
It let itself be gathered without fraying
And was no longer mist that clouds the air.
I stood, the valley once again surveying,   85
I saw the sky, it was sublimely fair.
And she, I saw, the purest veil was holding,
It flowed round her in myriad folds enfolding.

'I know you, know your weakness, your endeavour,
I know the good that lives and glows in you!'   90
Just so she spoke, I hear her words forever,
'Receive what I long marked out as your due!
The fortunate one knows deprivation never
Whose quiet soul accepts this gift anew:
From sunlight's clarity and scent of morning   95
By truth enwoven, poetry's veil adorning.

And when your friends and you look for some healing
From sultry noon, toss high this veil outspread!
An evening breeze, its cooling balm unsealing,
Shall breathe on you and flowers' essence shed.   100
Then shall subside all anxious earthly feeling,
The sombre vault become a cloudy bed,
The pounding waves of life be moderated,
The day grow sweet, the night illuminated!'

So come, my friends, when life for you seems blighted,   105
By burdens ever heavier oppressed,
Then when by flowers and golden fruits delighted
You find your path is once more newly blessed
To meet the next day we shall go united!
So we shall live, in happiness so quest.
And when our children mourn for us hereafter   110
Our love shall last to bring them joy and laughter.

An den Mond

(Spätere Fassung)

Füllest wieder Busch und Tal
Still mit Nebelglanz,
Lösest endlich auch einmal
Meine Seele ganz;

Breitest über mein Gefild   5
Lindernd deinen Blick,
Wie des Freundes Auge mild
Über mein Geschick.

Jeden Nachklang fühlt mein Herz
Froh- und trüber Zeit,   10
Wandle zwischen Freud' und Schmerz
In der Einsamkeit.

Fließe, fließe, lieber Fluß!
Nimmer werd' ich froh,
So verrauschte Scherz und Kuß,   15
Und die Treue so.

Ich besaß es doch einmal,
Was so köstlich ist!
Daß man doch zu seiner Qual
Nimmer es vergißt!   20

Rausche, Fluß, das Tal entlang,
Ohne Rast und Ruh,
Rausche, flüstre meinem Sang
Melodien zu,

Wenn du in der Winternacht   25
Wütend überschwillst,
Oder um die Frühlingspracht
Junger Knospen quillst.

Selig, wer sich vor der Welt
Ohne Haß verschließt,   30
Einen Freund am Busen hält
Und mit dem genießt,

Was, von Menschen nicht gewußt
Oder nicht bedacht,
Durch das Labyrinth der Brust   35
Wandelt in der Nacht.

To the Moon (1787–8)

(Later Version)

Filling wood and vale you cast
Quiet misty sheen,
And for once release at last
All my soul serene;

On my fields you spread your gaze   5
And alleviate,
As a dear friend's eye surveys
Gently all my fate.

Every glad and sad time's tone
My heart feels again,   10
I in solitude alone
Walk in joy and pain.

Dearest stream, flow on, flow on!
Joy I'll never know;
Just so jest and kiss are gone,   15
Faithfulness just so.

Once I really owned for sure
Sweetness haunting yet!
That we must the rack endure
Never to forget!   20

Downdale, stream, now rush along,
Restless ceaselessly
Rush, and whisper to my song
All your melody

When in winter you submerge   25
Night in raging floods,
Or in springtime when you surge
Round the bright young buds.

Bliss, to shut the world outside
Though no hate to bear,   30
And in one dear friend confide
And the pleasure share

That, by other men not known
Or not judged aright,
Roams the labyrinthine zone   35
Of the heart at night.

Römische Elegien

I

Saget, Steine, mir an, o sprecht, ihr hohen Paläste!
  Straßen, redet ein Wort! Genius, regst du dich nicht?
Ja, es ist alles beseelt in deinen heiligen Mauern,
  Ewige Roma; nur mir schweiget noch alles so still.
O wer flüstert mir zu, an welchem Fenster erblick' ich   5
  Einst das holde Geschöpf, das mich versengend erquickt?
Ahn' ich die Wege noch nicht, durch die ich immer und immer,
  Zu ihr und von ihr zu gehn, opfre die köstliche Zeit?
Noch betracht' ich Kirch' und Palast, Ruinen und Säulen,
  Wie ein bedächtiger Mann schicklich die Reise benutzt.   10
Doch bald ist es vorbei; dann wird ein einziger Tempel,
  Amors Tempel nur sein, der den Geweihten empfängt.
Eine Welt zwar bist du, o Rom; doch ohne die Liebe
  Wäre die Welt nicht die Welt, wäre denn Rom auch nicht Rom.

III

Laß dich, Geliebte, nicht reun, daß du mir so schnell dich ergeben!
  Glaub' es, ich denke nicht frech, denke nicht niedrig von dir.
Vielfach wirken die Pfeile des Amor: einige ritzen,
  Und vom schleichenden Gift kranket auf Jahre das Herz.
Aber mächtig befiedert, mit frisch geschliffener Schärfe   5
  Dringen die andern ins Mark, zünden behende das Blut.
In der heroischen Zeit, da Götter und Göttinnen liebten,
  Folgte Begierde dem Blick, folgte Genuß der Begier.
Glaubst du, es habe sich lange die Göttin der Liebe besonnen,
  Als im Idäischen Hain einst ihr Anchises gefiel?   10
Hätte Luna gesäumt, den schönen Schläfer zu küssen,
  O, so hätt' ihn geschwind, neidend, Aurora geweckt.
Hero erblickte Leandern am lauten Fest, und behende
  Stürzte der Liebende sich heiß in die nächtliche Flut.
Rhea Silvia wandelt, die fürstliche Jungfrau, der Tiber   15
  Wasser zu schöpfen, hinab, und sie ergreifet der Gott.
So erzeugte die Söhne sich Mars! – Die Zwillinge tränket
  Eine Wölfin, und Rom nennt sich die Fürstin der Welt.

V

Froh empfind' ich mich nun auf klassischem Boden begeistert,
  Vor- und Mitwelt spricht lauter und reizender mir.
Hier befolg' ich den Rat, durchblättre die Werke der Alten
  Mit geschäftiger Hand, täglich mit neuem Genuß.

Roman Elegies (1788–90)

I

Tell me, stones, and call out, O speak, you lofty palazzi!
    Streets, O talk to me now! Genius, will you not stir?
Yes, all is animate here within your sanctified ramparts,
    Rome everlasting; from me only its voice is withheld.
O, who whispers to me, and where's the window that lets me   5
    See that creature most fair whose fire shall freshen my life?
Have I not yet sensed those paths where I shall ever and ever,
    Going and coming from her, squander the treasure of time?
Still I gaze at palace and church, at ruins and columns,
    Serious-minded like one putting his tour to good use.   10
But soon all that is gone; then there'll be only one temple,
    Amor's temple alone, where the initiate's received.
You indeed are a world, O Rome; but failing love's presence
    World would not truly be world, nor then would Rome still be Rome.

III

Rue not, beloved, the haste that made you so swiftly surrender!
    Trust me, I don't think you base, mine are not insolent thoughts.
So diverse are the arrows of Amor: some just make scratches,
    And the poison that creeps sickens the heart year on year.
But with powerful pinions, and sharpened fresh from the whetstone,   5
    Others will pierce to the quick, cunningly fire the blood.
In the heroic age, when goddess or god had a passion
    Just one glance roused desire, straightway desire had its feast.
Think now, how long did love's goddess reflect and delay her decision
    Seeing Anchises' fair form there in the Idaen grove?   10
And had Luna delayed to kiss the beautiful sleeper
    Jealous Aurora for sure would quickly have kissed him awake.
Hero caught sight of Leander at the revels, and the lover
    Hurled himself hot from the feast into the nocturnal tide.
Rhea Silvia, princess and virgin, wanders down to the Tiber   15
    Meaning to draw some water, and there she's seized by the god.
Thus did Mars produce sons for himself! – The twin-born are suckled
    By a she-wolf, and Rome calls herself Queen of the World.

V

Now on classical ground I'm happy to sense it inspires me;
    Past and present speak louder, exciting me more.
Here I heed good advice, I leaf through the works of the ancients
    With assiduous hand, daily delighting anew.

Aber die Nächte hindurch hält Amor mich anders beschäftigt; 5
  Werd' ich auch halb nur gelehrt, bin ich doch doppelt beglückt.
Und belehr' ich mich nicht, indem ich des lieblichen Busens
  Formen spähe, die Hand leite die Hüften hinab?
Dann versteh' ich den Marmor erst recht: ich denk' und vergleiche,
  Sehe mit fühlendem Aug', fühle mit sehender Hand. 10
Raubt die Liebste denn gleich mir einige Stunden des Tages,
  Gibt sie Stunden der Nacht mir zur Entschädigung hin.
Wird doch nicht immer geküßt, es wird vernünftig gesprochen;
  Überfällt sie der Schlaf, lieg' ich und denke mir viel.
Oftmals hab' ich auch schon in ihren Armen gedichtet 15
  Und des Hexameters Maß leise mit fingernder Hand
Ihr auf den Rücken gezählt. Sie atmet in lieblichem Schlummer,
  Und es durchglühet ihr Hauch mir bis ins Tiefste die Brust.
Amor schüret die Lamp' indes und denket der Zeiten,
  Da er den nämlichen Dienst seinen Triumvirn getan. 20

VII

O wie fühl' ich in Rom mich so froh! gedenk' ich der Zeiten,
  Da mich ein graulicher Tag hinten im Norden umfing,
Trübe der Himmel und schwer auf meine Scheitel sich senkte,
  Farb- und gestaltlos die Welt um den Ermatteten lag,
Und ich über mein Ich, des unbefriedigten Geistes 5
  Düstre Wege zu spähn, still in Betrachtung versank.
Nun umleuchtet der Glanz des helleren Äthers die Stirne;
  Phöbus rufet, der Gott, Formen und Farben hervor.
Sternhell glänzet die Nacht, sie klingt von weichen Gesängen,
  Und mir leuchtet der Mond heller als nordischer Tag. 10
Welche Seligkeit ward mir Sterblichem! Träum' ich? Empfänget
  Dein ambrosisches Haus, Jupiter Vater, den Gast?
Ach! hier lieg' ich und strecke nach deinen Knieen die Hände
  Flehend aus. O vernimm, Jupiter Xenius, mich!
Wie ich hereingekommen, ich kann's nicht sagen; es faßte 15
  Hebe den Wandrer und zog mich in die Hallen heran.
Hast du ihr einen Heroen herauf zu führen geboten?
  Irrte die Schöne? Vergib! Laß mir des Irrtums Gewinn!
Deine Tochter Fortuna, sie auch! die herrlichsten Gaben
  Teilt als ein Mädchen sie aus, wie es die Laune gebeut. 20
Bist du der wirtliche Gott? O dann so verstoße den Gastfreund
  Nicht von deinem Olymp wieder zur Erde hinab!
'Dichter! wohin versteigest du dich?' – Vergib mir; der hohe
  Kapitolinische Berg ist dir ein zweiter Olymp.

But when it comes to the nights I'm otherwise busied by Amor;   5
   And if I'm only half-taught doubly I'm happy instead.
And don't I teach myself by watching the bosom's endearing
   Forms that charm me, my hands gliding below down the hips?
Then I really know marble at last: I think in comparing,
   See with the eye as it feels, feel with the hand as it sees.   10
Though my love may be stealing some of the hours from my daytime
   She gives full compensation in the hours of night.
Not that it's kissing alone, there's also sensible talking;
   When she's fallen asleep I will just lie and reflect.
Often too in her arms I lay and worked out a poem;   15
   Counting hexameter's length, softly my fingering hand
Measured it out on her back. She breathes in the sweetest of slumbers,
   And I am warmed by her breath glowing all through me within.
Amor trims up the lamp meanwhile and thinks of that era
   When he performed that same task serving his Triumvirate.[5]   20

VII

O how happy my feelings in Rome! to think what I lived through,
   Back there up North, when the days held me in greyness enclosed,
Skies sinking down on my head, sombre and heavily pressing,
   Round me, exhausted, the world all without colour and form,
When I delved through my mind to trace in silent reflection   5
   How my unappeased self floundered on darkening paths.
Now this ether-bright light illumines my brow with its radiance;
   Forms and colours spring forth, summoned by Phoebus the god;
Night is starbright aglow, with song is gently melodious,
   And the moon shines for me brighter than day in the North.   10
Me, a mortal, what bliss was given to me! Dreams? Am I now in
   Your ambrosial house, Jupiter Father, your guest?
Ah, I lie here before you in supplication and raise my
   Outstretched hands. Hear my plea, Jupiter Xenius, hear!
Really I can't explain it, the way I got here; but Hebe   15
   Came to the wanderer and brought me here to enter your halls.
Did you give her the instruction to bring a hero as guest here?
   Was she in error? Forgive! Let me keep error's reward!
And your daughter Fortuna, she too! a girl who disburses
   Marvellous gifts by whim just as her fancy dictates.   20
Are you the god of all guests? O banish him not from Olympus,
   Do not send back the guest once more to earth down below! –
'Poet! You climb too high from your place!' – Forgive me; the rising
   Hill of the Capitol forms a second Olympus for you.

Dulde mich, Jupiter, hier, und Hermes führe mich später, 25
    Cestius' Mal vorbei, leise zum Orkus hinab.

XV

Cäsarn wär' ich wohl nie zu fernen Britannen gefolget,
    Florus hätte mich leicht in die Popine geschleppt!
Denn mir bleiben weit mehr die Nebel des traurigen Nordens
    Als ein geschäftiges Volk südlicher Flöhe verhaßt.
Und noch schöner von heut' an seid mir gegrüßet, ihr Schenken, 5
    Osterien, wie euch schicklich der Römer benennt;
Denn ihr zeigtet mir heute die Liebste, begleitet vom Oheim,
    Den die Gute so oft, mich zu besitzen, betrügt.
Hier stand unser Tisch, den Deutsche vertraulich umgaben;
    Drüben suchte das Kind neben der Mutter den Platz, 10
Rückte vielmals die Bank und wußt' es artig zu machen,
    Daß ich halb ihr Gesicht, völlig den Nacken gewann.
Lauter sprach sie, als hier die Römerin pfleget, kredenzte,
    Blickte gewendet nach mir, goß und verfehlte das Glas.
Wein floß über den Tisch, und sie, mit zierlichem Finger, 15
    Zog auf dem hölzernen Blatt Kreise der Feuchtigkeit hin.
Meinen Namen verschlang sie dem ihrigen; immer begierig
    Schaut' ich dem Fingerchen nach, und sie bemerkte mich wohl.
Endlich zog sie behende das Zeichen der römischen Fünfe
    Und ein Strichlein davor. Schnell, und sobald ich's gesehn, 20
Schlang sie Kreise durch Kreise, die Lettern und Ziffern zu löschen;
    Aber die köstliche Vier blieb mir ins Auge geprägt.
Stumm war ich sitzen geblieben und biß die glühende Lippe,
    Halb aus Schalkheit und Lust, halb aus Begierde, mir wund.
Erst noch so lange bis Nacht! dann noch vier Stunden zu warten! 25
    Hohe Sonne, du weilst, und du beschauest dein Rom!
Größeres sahest du nichts und wirst nichts Größeres sehen,
    Wie es dein Priester Horaz in der Entzückung versprach.
Aber heute verweile mir nicht, und wende die Blicke
    Von dem Siebengebirg früher und williger ab! 30
Einem Dichter zuliebe verkürze die herrlichen Stunden,
    Die mit begierigem Blick selig der Maler genießt;
Glühend blicke noch schnell zu diesen hohen Fassaden,
    Kuppeln und Säulen zuletzt und Obelisken herauf;
Stürze dich eilig ins Meer, um morgen früher zu sehen, 35
    Was Jahrhunderte schon göttliche Lust dir gewährt:

Jupiter, bear with me here, and afterwards lead me hereafter 25
    Down past Cestius's tomb gently to Orcus below.

XV

I would never have gone and marched after Caesar to Britain,
    Florus would have easily dragged me away and off to the pub!
For the mists of the North are sad and by far the more hateful
    Than the assiduous fleas swarming all over the South.
And I'll greet you more warmly from this day onwards, you taverns, 5
    Osterie, as so aptly you're called here in Rome;
For you showed me my darling today, with her uncle beside her
    Whom she often deceives so she can have me again.
Here our table stood, familiar with Germans around it;
    There by her mother's seat, that's where the child found a place, 10
Often shifting the bench, with graceful manners contriving
    That I saw half her face and the full view of her neck.
Louder than normal for Roman women she talked, raised the bottle,
    Turned round and looked towards me, poured and the wine missed her glass.
Wine flowed over the board and she, with neat dainty finger, 15
    Drew on the table's leaf circling lines from the wet.
My and her name she tangled together there; I kept my avid
    Eyes on her finger's quick moves, and she observed that I did.
Nimbly ending she added a Five in the script of the Romans
    And in front put a stroke. Quick, when I'd seen, she rubbed, 20
Winding circles through circles to blot out the letters and numbers;
    But that most exquisite *Four* stayed as if stamped in my eyes.
I remained silent and sat there and bit my lip till it hurt me,
    Half in pleasure and tease, half in the pangs of desire.
First the long wait until night! and then still four hours of waiting! 25
    Sun resplendent, you pause, gazing a while on your Rome!
You have seen nothing more great and won't see anything greater,
    As was foretold by your priest, Horace, in thrills of delight.
But today don't linger at all and cut short your looking,
    Leave the sevenfold hills earlier and readier for once! 30
For the sake of a poet curtail the fine splendour of hours
    Painters enjoy with an eye raptured and greeding for more;
Let your last glowing look be quick to climb these facades now,
    Up over columns and domes and obelisks up and up;
Hurl yourself into the sea, to view the quicker tomorrow 35
    What for centuries now gives you the pleasure of gods:

Diese feuchten, mit Rohr so lange bewachsnen Gestade,
    Diese mit Bäumen und Busch düster beschatteten Höhn.
Wenig Hütten zeigten sie erst; dann sahst du auf einmal
    Sie vom wimmelnden Volk glücklicher Räuber belebt.   40
Alles schleppten sie drauf an diese Stätte zusammen;
    Kaum war das übrige Rund deiner Betrachtung noch wert.
Sahst eine Welt hier entstehn, sahst dann eine Welt hier in Trümmern,
    Aus den Trümmern aufs neu fast eine größere Welt!
Daß ich diese noch lange von dir beleuchtet erblicke,   45
    Spinne die Parze mir klug langsam den Faden herab.
Aber sie eile herbei, die schön bezeichnete Stunde! –
    Glücklich! hör' ich sie schon? Nein, doch ich höre schon Drei.
So, ihr lieben Musen, betrogt ihr wieder die Länge
    Dieser Weile, die mich von der Geliebten getrennt.   50
Lebet wohl! Nun eil' ich und fürcht' euch nicht zu beleid'gen:
    Denn ihr Stolzen, ihr gebt Amorn doch immer den Rang.

Venezianische Epigramme

I

Sarkophagen und Urnen verzierte der Heide mit Leben:
    Faunen tanzen umher, mit der Bacchantinnen Chor
Machen sie bunte Reihe; der ziegengefüßete Pausback
    Zwingt den heiseren Ton wild aus dem schmetternden Horn.
Zimbeln, Trommeln erklingen; wir sehen und hören den Marmor.   5
    Flatternde Vögel! wie schmeckt herrlich dem Schnabel die Frucht!
Euch verscheuchet kein Lärm, noch weniger scheucht er den Amor,
    Der in dem bunten Gewühl erst sich der Fackel erfreut.
So überwältiget Fülle den Tod; und die Asche da drinnen
    Scheint, im stillen Bezirk, noch sich des Lebens zu freun.   10
So umgebe denn spät den Sarkophagen des Dichters
    Diese Rolle, von ihm reichlich mit Leben geschmückt.

VIII

Diese Gondel vergleich' ich der Wiege, sie schaukelt gefällig,
    Und das Kästchen darauf scheint ein geräumiger Sarg.
Recht so! Zwischen der Wieg und dem Sarg wir schwanken und schweben
    Auf dem großen Kanal sorglos durchs Leben dahin.

XXXVI

Müde war ich geworden, nur immer Gemälde zu sehen,
    Herrliche Schätze der Kunst, wie sie Venedig bewahrt.

Marshy banks here, where serried reeds have been growing for ages,
    Here all around the dark hills, shaded by bushes and trees.
First they showed but very few huts; then one day you saw them
    Spring to life as the race of fortunate plunderers swarmed.   40
All was booty to them and all was dragged to this city,
    So that the rest of the globe hardly deserved that you looked.
Here first you saw a new world, and then saw a world here in ruins,
    Then from ruins once more almost a still greater world!
So that I may see this one beneath your light for much longer   45
    Grant me that Clotho be slow spinning the thread of my life;
But let that one thing come quick, that hour so prettily signalled! –
    Happy! Did it just strike? No; but already it's Three.
Thus, beloved Muses, once more you came and beguiled me,
    Charmed away this long wait whilst I'm apart from my love.   50
Now farewell! I hurry and know I do not offend you;
    For, though proud, you agree Amor has always first place.

Venetian Epigrams (1790)

I

Sarcophagus, ampulla, the pagan chose life to adorn them:
    Fauns are dancing about, making a gaudy bright ring
With the Bacchantes' chorus; that goat-footed one of a fat-face
    Blasts the throaty hoarse notes wild from his shattering horn.
Cymbals, tambours are clanging; we see and we hear in the marble.   5
    Birds in a flutter! that fruit, splendid it tastes to the beak!
You're not scared off by noise, still less can it frighten off Amor,
    Needing a revelling crowd if he's to play with his torch.
Thus by abundance is death overcome; and the ashes inside them
    Seem, in silence enclosed, still to rejoice in this life.   10
Thus let this later scroll enwrap the tomb of the poet,
    These inscriptions of his, patterned so richly with life.

VIII

See this gondola like to a cradle rocking so gently,
    And the casket on top seems like a coffin with room.
Just so! In between cradle and coffin we haver and hover
    Here on life's grand canal thoughtlessly floating along.

XXXVI

I was sated and weary with looking at paintings forever,
    Marvellous treasures of art such as in Venice abound.

Denn auch dieser Genuß verlangt Erholung und Muße;
    Nach lebendigem Reiz suchte mein schmachtender Blick.
Gauklerin! da ersah ich in dir zu den Bübchen das Urbild,   5
    Wie sie Johannes Bellin reizend mit Flügeln gemalt,
Wie sie Paul Veronese mit Bechern dem Bräutigam sendet,
    Dessen Gäste, getäuscht, Wasser genießen für Wein.

XXXVII

Wie, von der künstlichsten Hand geschnitzt, das liebe Figürchen,
    Weich und ohne Gebein, wie die Molluska nur schwimmt!
Alles ist Glied, und alles Gelenk, und alles gefällig,
    Alles nach Maßen gebaut, alles nach Willkür bewegt.
Menschen hab ich gekannt und Tiere, so Vögel als Fische,   5
    Manches besondre Gewürm, Wunder der großen Natur;
Und doch staun ich dich an, Bettine, liebliches Wunder,
    Die du alles zugleich bist, und ein Engel dazu.

XLI

So verwirret mit dumpf willkürlich verwebten Gestalten,
    Höllisch und trübe gesinnt, Breughel den schwankenden Blick;
So zerrüttet auch Dürer mit apokalyptischen Bildern,
    Menschen und Grillen zugleich, unser gesundes Gehirn;
So erreget ein Dichter, von Sphinxen, Sirenen, Zentauren   5
    Singend, die Neugier mit Macht in dem verwunderten Ohr;
So beweget ein Traum den Sorglichen, wenn er zu greifen,
    Vorwärts glaubet zu gehn, alles veränderlich schwebt:
So verwirrt uns Bettine, die holden Glieder verwechselnd;
    Doch erfreut sie uns gleich, wenn sie die Sohlen betritt.   10

XLII

Gern überschreit ich die Grenze, mit breiter Kreide gezogen.
    Macht sie Bottegha, das Kind, drängt sie mich artig zurück.

XLIV

Alles seh ich so gerne von dir; doch seh ich am liebsten,
    Wenn der Vater behend über dich selber dich wirft,
Du dich im Schwung überschlägst und, nach dem tödlichen Sprunge,
    Wieder stehest und läufst, eben ob nichts wär geschehn.

XLVII

'Welch ein Wahnsinn ergriff dich Müßigen? Hältst du nicht inne?
    Wird dies Mädchen ein Buch? Stimme was Klügeres an!'
Wartet, ich singe die Könige bald, die Großen der Erde,
    Wenn ich ihr Handwerk einst besser begreife wie jetzt.

From this pleasure as well some rest and recovery's needed;
  And my languishing eye looked for some living delight.
Sorceress! then I could see in you those cherubims' model,   5
  Just like Bellini portrays, painted with wings that enchant,
Just as Paul Veronese will send them with cups to the bridegroom
  And to the guests who enjoy, deluded, the water as wine.

XXXVII

How, from an exquisite artist's hand, the dear little figure,
  Soft and without any bones, mollusc-like simply swims!
Everything's limb, and everything's joint, and everything's pleasing,
  Everything measured to scale, everything moves as it wills.
Many humans I've known, and animals, birds, many fishes,   5
  Many peculiar reptiles, great nature's marvellous works;
And yet I'm astonished by you, Bettina, dearest of marvels,
  You who are all things at once, and an angel as well.

XLI

So will Breughel with figures tangled by primitive whimsy,
  Hellish and sombre in mood, muddle our wavering sight;
So will Dürer convulse us with apocalyptic pictures,
  Humans and fancies combined, sapping the health of our brains;
So a poet excites us, of sphinxes and sirens and centaurs   5
  Singing, will maze wonders and will astonish the ear;
So a dream will disturb the careful one; thinking of holding,
  Stepping straight on ahead, all tilts unstable and sways:
So Bettina confuses, her beauteous limbs all a-changing;
  But we're instantly glad when she steps back on her feet.   10

XLII

How I'd exceed all the limits, outlined in chalk quite distinctly.
  When she's performing the child courteously pushes me back.

XLIV

I like to watch all the things that you do; but best I like watching
  When your father, adroit, tosses you head over heels,
You turning somersaults fly and from the salto mortale
  Once more stand up and run, just as if nothing had been.

XLVII

'What's this madness that's hit your indolence? Why don't you stop it?
  Shall this girl be a book? Play a more sensible tune!'
Patience, I'll sing about kings very soon, the world and its great ones,
  Once I can grasp their craft better than now I can do.

Doch Bettinen sing ich indes; denn Gaukler und Dichter   5
  Sind gar nahe verwandt, suchen und finden sich gern.

LXVIII

Wer Lazerten gesehn, der kann sich die zierlichen Mädchen
  Denken, die über den Platz fahren dahin und daher.
Schnell und beweglich sind sie, und gleiten, stehen und schwatzen,
  Und es rauscht das Gewand hinter den eilenden drein.
Sieh, hier ist sie! und hier! Verlierst du sie einmal, so suchst du   5
  Sie vergebens; so bald kommt sie nicht wieder hervor.
Wenn du aber die Winkel, die Gäßchen und Treppchen nicht scheuest,
  Folg ihr, wie sie dich lockt, in die Spelunke hinein!

LXX

Zwei der feinsten Lazerten, sie hielten sich immer zusammen,
  Eine beinahe zu groß, eine beinahe zu klein.
Siehst du beide zusammen, so wird die Wahl dir unmöglich;
  Jede besonders, sie schien einzig die schönste zu sein.

LXXVII

Mit Botanik gibst du dich ab? mit Optik? Was tust du?
  Ist es nicht schönrer Gewinn, rühren ein zärtliches Herz?
Ach, die zärtlichen Herzen! ein Pfuscher vermag sie zu rühren;
  Sei es mein einziges Glück, dich zu berühren, Natur!

XC

Welch ein lustiges Spiel! Es windet am Faden die Scheibe,
  Die von der Hand entfloh, eilig sich wieder herauf!
Seht, so schein ich mein Herz bald dieser Schönen, bald jener
  Zuzuwerfen; doch gleich kehrt es im Fluge zurück.

XCV

Du erstaunest, und zeigst mir das Meer; es scheinet zu brennen.
  Wie bewegt sich die Flut flammend ums nächtliche Schiff!
Mich verwundert es nicht, das Meer gebar Aphroditen,
  Und entsprang nicht aus ihr uns eine Flamme, der Sohn?

CII

Wonniglich ist's, die Geliebte verlangend im Arme zu halten,
  Wenn ihr klopfendes Herz Liebe zuerst dir gesteht.
Wonniglicher, das Pochen des Neulebendigen fühlen,
  Das in dem lieblichen Schoß immer sich nährend bewegt.
Schon versucht es die Sprünge der raschen Jugend; es klopfet   5
  Ungeduldig schon an, sehnt sich nach himmlischem Licht.

But for now Bettina's my song; for jugglers and poets   5
   Are so closely akin, seek out and find their own kind.

LXVIII

Think of lizards you've seen to picture the exquisite girls there
   Rightly, all over the square moving now here and now there.
Quick and mercurial they are and gliding, standing and chatting,
   And there's rustle of skirt trailed as they hurry away.
Look, she's there now! and there! If once you should lose her it's
     useless   5
   To keep seeking; she won't come back so quickly again.
If however you fear no dark nooks, nor alleys and stairways,
   Go then, follow her lure, where the tavern invites!

LXX

Lizards, two of the finest, would always walk out with each other;
   One of them almost too big, one of them almost too small.
If you see them together you can't choose one or the other;
   Each one alone though appeared clearly the loveliest of all.

LXXVII

'Botanising passing your time? with optics? What's that for?
   Are there not nicer rewards touching the sensitive hearts?'
Ah, the sensitive hearts now! a bungler is able to touch them;
   Let this alone be my joy, Nature, to touch all of you!

XC

What a tease of a game! The disc on the thread is revolving,
   Out of the hand escaped quickly it climbs back again!
See, it seems like my heart, to this fair beauty then that one
   I may throw it; but then back in an instant it flies.

XCV

You're amazed and you point out the sea; it seems to be burning.
   How the waves flood in flames here round the ship in the night!
I'm by no means surprised; the ocean bore Aphrodite,
   And from her leaped to us surely a flame, her son?

CII

It's a delight, to be holding your love in your arms with her longing
   Whilst the beat of her heart newly confesses her love.
Still more delight, to feel how the new live being is thumping
   As it incessantly moves feeding within the sweet womb.
Even now like impetuous youth it's jumping; already   5
   How impatient it knocks, longs to reach heavenly light.

Harre noch wenige Tage! Auf allen Pfaden des Lebens
Führen die Horen dich streng, wie es das Schicksal gebeut.
Widerfahre dir, was dir auch will, du wachsender Liebling –
Liebe bildete dich; werde dir Liebe zuteil!   10

CIII
Und so tändelt ich mir, von allen Freuden geschieden,
In der Neptunischen Stadt Tage wie Stunden hinweg.
Alles, was ich erfuhr, ich würzt es mit süßer Erinnrung,
Würzt es mit Hoffnung; sie sind lieblichste Würzen der Welt.

Aus dem Nachlass

XLI
Köstliche Ringe besitz ich! Gegrabne fürtreffliche Steine
Hoher Gedanken und Stils fasset ein lauteres Gold.
Teurer bezahlt man die Ringe geschmückt mit feurigen Steinen,
Blinken hast du sie oft über dem Spieltisch gesehn.
Aber ein Ringelchen kenn ich, das hat sich anders gewaschen,   5
Das Hans Carvel einmal traurig im Alter besaß.
Unklug schob er den kleinsten der zehen Finger ins Ringchen,
Nur der größte gehört, würdig, der elfte, hinein.

LXX
In dem engsten der Gäßchen – es drängte sich kaum durch die Mauern –
Saß mir ein Mädchen im Weg, als ich Venedig durchlief.
Sie war reizend, der Ort, ich ließ mich Fremder verführen;
Ach, ein weiter Kanal tat sich dem Forschenden auf.
Hättest du Mädchen wie deine Kanäle, Venedig und F ...   5
Wie die Gäßchen in dir, wärst du die herrlichste Stadt.

Nähe des Geliebten

Ich denke dein, wenn mir der Sonne Schimmer
    Vom Meere strahlt;
Ich denke dein, wenn sich des Mondes Flimmer
    In Quellen malt.

Ich sehe dich, wenn auf dem fernen Wege   5
    Der Staub sich hebt;
In tiefer Nacht, wenn auf dem schmalen Stege
    Der Wandrer bebt.

Wait just a few more days longer! The Horae soon enough lead you
   Strictly through all of life's paths, following Fate's stern command.
Whatsoever befall you in time, you dear little thriveling –
   You were fashioned by Love; Love be your portion in life!   10

CIII

Thus I dallied with time, cut off from friends to divert me,
   In the Neptunian town losing the hours and days.
All I experienced I spiced with my sweet recollections,
   Spiced it with hope; they're the most exquisite spice in the world.

Withheld Venetian Epigrams
XLI

Exquisite rings I have purchased! Engraved and most excellent crystals,
   Noble in style as in theme, clasped in the purest of gold.
Dearly those rings must be paid for that flash with the blazing of crystals
   Such as often you've seen aglow on the gambling board.
But there's a ringlet I know of, that's quite a different story,   5
   One Hans Carvel[6] when old one time so sadly possessed.
He unwisely the smallest of all his ten fingers inserted
   There where worthily fits only the biggest, eleven.

LXX

In the narrowest alley – a slip one hardly could squeeze through –
   Blocking my way sat a girl, when I walked Venice one day.
Fired by her, and the place, a stranger I then lost my bearings;
   Oh, how wide a canal opened for me to explore.
If you had girls like canals that you offer, O Venice, and c—s   5
   Like your alleys within, you'd be a city supreme.

Lover's Nearness (1796)

I think of you, whenever sun's bright shimmer
From ocean streams;
I think of you, whenever moon's soft glimmer
In wellsprings gleams.

I see you when, there on the distant ridgeway,   5
The dust-cloud blurs;
In deepest night, when on the narrow bridgeway
The wanderer stirs.

Ich höre dich, wenn dort mit dumpfem Rauschen
    Die Welle steigt.   10
Im stillen Haine geh' ich oft zu lauschen,
    Wenn alles schweigt.

Ich bin bei dir, du seist auch noch so ferne,
    Du bist mir nah!
Die Sonne sinkt, bald leuchten mir die Sterne.   15
    O wärst du da!

Der Gott und die Bajadere

Indische Legende

Mahadöh, der Herr der Erde,
Kommt herab zum sechsten Mal,
Daß er unsersgleichen werde,
Mit zu fühlen Freud' und Qual.
Er bequemt sich, hier zu wohnen,   5
Läßt sich alles selbst geschehn.
Soll er strafen oder schonen,
Muß er Menschen menschlich sehn.
Und hat er die Stadt sich als Wandrer betrachtet,
Die Großen belauert, auf Kleine geachtet,   10
Verläßt er sie abends, um weiter zu gehn.

Als er nun hinausgegangen,
Wo die letzten Häuser sind,
Sieht er mit gemalten Wangen
Ein verlornes schönes Kind.   15
'Grüß' dich, Jungfrau!' – 'Dank der Ehre!
Wart', ich komme gleich hinaus.' –
'Und wer bist du?' – 'Bajadere,
Und dies ist der Liebe Haus.'
Sie rührt sich, die Cymbeln zum Tanze zu schlagen;   20
Sie weiß sich so lieblich im Kreise zu tragen,
Sie neigt sich und biegt sich und reicht ihm den Strauß.

Schmeichelnd zieht sie ihn zur Schwelle,
Lebhaft ihn ins Haus hinein.
'Schöner Fremdling, lampenhelle   25
Soll sogleich die Hütte sein.
Bist du müd', ich will dich laben,

I hear you in the muffled sound of surging
When tide-wave fills; 10
In quiet grove I listen to the urging
When silence stills.

I am with you, though you be far and pining,
You are so near!
The sun goes down. The stars will soon be shining. 15
Would you were here!

The God and the Bayadere (1797)

Indian Legend

Lord of Earth, great Mahadeva,
Comes a sixth time down again,
Comes to feel with each believer
All our human joy and pain.
Here to dwell with us he pleases 5
To experience come what may.
As he punishes or eases
Mankind's lot he must essay.
And when in the town his inspection he's ended,
Has spied on the great, to the humble attended, 10
He leaves it at evening to go on his way.

When at very last he reaches
Houses on the city's bourn
There he sees the painted features
Of a lovely child forlorn. 15
'Greetings, Mistress!' – 'Praise I treasure!
I'll come out, do stay with me.' –
'Say who are you?' – 'Girl of pleasure;
This the house of love you see.'
She starts on her dance to the beat of the cymbal, 20
She graces the space as she circles so nimble,
She finely inclines as she ends on her knee.

To the threshold, charming sprightly,
To the house she leads him through.
'Stranger fair, soon lamplight-brightly 25
All this room will shine for you.
If you're tired I'll revive you,

Lindern deiner Füße Schmerz.
Was du willst, das sollst du haben,
Ruhe, Freuden oder Scherz.'   30
Sie lindert geschäftig geheuchelte Leiden.
Der Göttliche lächelt; er siehet mit Freuden
Durch tiefes Verderben ein menschliches Herz.

Und er fordert Sklavendienste;
Immer heitrer wird sie nur,   35
Und des Mädchens frühe Künste
Werden nach und nach Natur.
Und so stellet auf die Blüte
Bald und bald die Frucht sich ein;
Ist Gehorsam im Gemüte,   40
Wird nicht fern die Liebe sein.
Aber sie schärfer und schärfer zu prüfen,
Wählet der Kenner der Höhen und Tiefen
Lust und Entsetzen und grimmige Pein.

Und er küßt die bunten Wangen,   45
Und sie fühlt der Liebe Qual,
Und das Mädchen steht gefangen,
Und sie weint zum ersten Mal;
Sinkt zu seinen Füßen nieder,
Nicht um Wollust noch Gewinst,   50
Ach, und die gelenken Glieder,
Sie versagen allen Dienst.
Und so zu des Lagers vergnüglicher Feier
Bereiten den dunklen behaglichen Schleier
Die nächtlichen Stunden das schöne Gespinst.   55

Spät entschlummert unter Scherzen,
Früh erwacht nach kurzer Rast,
Findet sie an ihrem Herzen
Tot den vielgeliebten Gast.
Schreiend stürzt sie auf ihn nieder;   60
Aber nicht erweckt sie ihn,
Und man trägt die starren Glieder
Bald zur Flammengrube hin.
Sie höret die Priester, die Totengesänge,
Sie raset und rennet und teilet die Menge.   65
'Wer bist du? was drängt zu der Grube dich hin?'

Soothe and ease your feet that smart.
All your wants, I'll not deprive you,
Rest, or zest, or jest impart.'   30
The pains he pretends to she's quickly relieving.
The god looks on smiling, with pleasure perceiving
In depth of corruption so human a heart.

Slave-girl duties he arranges
But she only grows more gay,   35
And what was her art now changes
By and by to nature's way.
So the flower boomed and fruited,
Naturally her gifts appear:
Where obedience is rooted   40
Love as well is very near.
But testing her closer more sharp ways he uses,
Heights and the depths he knows well and he chooses
Pleasure and terror and torments to fear.

On daubed cheeks his kisses showered,   45
And she feels a love that sears,
And the girl stands overpowered
And the first time she sheds tears;
At his feet she sinks down humbly,
Not for lust, and not for gain;   50
Ah, the limbs once lithe and comely
Fail her as her spirits wane.
Then hours of the night for the deep consummation
Spread softly a veil round the sweet celebration
In loveliness spun from their ample dark skein.   55

Late to sleep, with heart's tease vying,
Waking early from short rest
Close beside her she finds lying
Dead her dearest much-loved guest.
And her screams cannot restore him   60
As she clasps her heart's desire;
Cold and rigid he, they bore him
Swiftly to the funeral fire.
She hears the intoning, the priests and the dirges,
In frenzy she thrusts through the crowd as it surges.   65
'Who are you? By what right are you at the pyre?'

Bei der Bahre stürzt sie nieder,
Ihr Geschrei durchdringt die Luft:
'Meinen Gatten will ich wieder!
Und ich such' ihn in der Gruft.   70
Soll zu Asche mir zerfallen
Dieser Glieder Götterpracht?
Mein! er war es, mein vor allen!
Ach, nur Eine süße Nacht!'
Es singen die Priester: 'Wir tragen die Alten,   75
Nach langem Ermatten und spätem Erkalten,
Wir tragen die Jugend, noch eh' sie's gedacht.

Höre deiner Priester Lehre:
Dieser war dein Gatte nicht.
Lebst du doch als Bajadere,
Und so hast du keine Pflicht.   80
Nur dem Körper folgt der Schatten
In das stille Totenreich;
Nur die Gattin folgt dem Gatten:
Das ist Pflicht und Ruhm zugleich.   85
Ertöne, Drommete, zu heiliger Klage!
O nehmet, ihr Götter! die Zierde der Tage,
O nehmet den Jüngling in Flammen zu euch!'

So das Chor, das ohn' Erbarmen
Mehret ihres Herzens Not;   90
Und mit ausgestreckten Armen
Springt sie in den heißen Tod.
Doch der Götterjüngling hebet
Aus der Flamme sich empor,
Und in seinen Armen schwebet   95
Die Geliebte mit hervor.
Es freut sich die Gottheit der reuigen Sünder;
Unsterbliche heben verlorene Kinder
Mit feurigen Armen zum Himmel empor.

By the bier she falls down shrieking,
Cries that pierce through all the sky:
'This my husband I am seeking!
Give him back, I tomb defy. 70
Shall these limbs be ash and smother,
This divine and splendid sight?
Mine! he was! for no one other!
Oh, for only One sweet night!'
The priests go on chanting: 'The aged are taken, 75
Long wearied and finally cold and forsaken,
The young ones are taken surprised in full flight.

Hear your priests and hear our ruling:
This was not your husband true.
Bayadere are you by schooling 80
So no duty lies on you.
Only shade with corpse united
Rights in death's hushed realm can claim,
Only wife to husband plighted:
That is duty, that is fame. 85
Sound, trumpet, the sacred and sad lamentation!
O gods, take this jewel of time's brief duration,
O take to your keeping the youth in this flame!'

Ruthless chorus, that augmented
Anguish in her every breath; 90
Arms outstretched she leaps tormented
To the burning blaze of death.
But the god-youth freely soaring
From the flames ascends the sky;
With him, in his arms restoring, 95
His beloved floats on high.
For penitent sinners divinity jubilates;
Immortals lift children of darkness that desolates
In burning embraces to heaven on high.

Die Metamorphose der Pflanzen

Dich verwirret, Geliebte, die tausendfältige Mischung
  Diese Blumengewühls, über dem Garten umher;
Viele Namen hörest du an, und immer verdränget
  Mit barbarischem Klang einer den andern im Ohr.
Alle Gestalten sind ähnlich, und keine gleichet der andern;   5
  Und so deutet das Chor auf ein geheimes Gesetz,
Auf ein heiliges Rätsel. O könnt' ich dir, liebliche Freundin,
  Überliefern sogleich glücklich das lösende Wort!
Werdend betrachte sie nun, wie nach und nach sich die Pflanze,
  Stufenweise geführt, bildet zu Blüten und Frucht.   10
Aus dem Samen entwickelt sie sich, sobald ihn der Erde
  Stille befruchtender Schoß hold in das Leben entläßt,
Und dem Reize des Lichts, des heiligen, ewig bewegten,
  Gleich den zärtesten Bau keimender Blätter empfiehlt.
Einfach schlief in dem Samen die Kraft; ein beginnendes Vorbild 15
  Lag, verschlossen in sich, unter die Hülle gebeugt,
Blatt und Wurzel und Keim, nur halb geformet und farblos;
  Trocken erhält so der Kern ruhiges Leben bewahrt,
Quillet strebend empor, sich milder Feuchte vertrauend,
  Und erhebt sich sogleich aus der umgebenden Nacht.   20
Aber einfach bleibt die Gestalt der ersten Erscheinung;
  Und so bezeichnet sich auch unter den Pflanzen das Kind.
Gleich darauf ein folgender Trieb, sich erhebend, erneuet,
  Knoten auf Knoten getürmt, immer das erste Gebild.
Zwar nicht immer das gleiche; denn mannigfaltig erzeugt sich,   25
  Ausgebildet, du siehst's, immer das folgende Blatt,
Ausgedehnter, gekerbter, getrennter in Spitzen und Teile,
  Die verwachsen vorher ruhten im untern Organ.
Und so erreicht es zuerst die höchst bestimmte Vollendung,
  Die bei manchem Geschlecht dich zum Erstaunen bewegt.   30
Viel gerippt und gezackt, auf mastig strotzender Fläche,
  Scheinet die Fülle des Triebs frei und unendlich zu sein.
Doch hier hält die Natur, mit mächtigen Händen, die Bildung
  An und lenket sie sanft in das Vollkommnere hin.
Mäßiger leitet sie nun den Saft, verengt die Gefäße,   35
  Und gleich zeigt die Gestalt zärtere Wirkungen an.
Stille zieht sich der Trieb der strebenden Ränder zurücke,
  Und die Rippe des Stiels bildet sich völliger aus.
Blattlos aber und schnell erhebt sich der zärtere Stengel,
  Und ein Wundergebild zieht den Betrachtenden an.   40

The Metamorphosis of Plants (June 1798)

This confuses you, dearest, these modes of thousands of minglings
   In the riotous flowers spread through the garden all round;
Many names you hear with respect, and each one's barbaric
   Sound will always displace each that you heard just before.
All forms are like in their structure, and none equates with the other; 5
   And this common accord points to mysterious law,
To a sacred enigma. O could I, my dearest companion,
   Give you one happy word apt to resolve all at once!
Watch as it comes into being, see how the plant through progression,
   Guided step-wise along, forms into flowers and fruit.   10
It develops at once from the seed as soon as the quiet
   Life-giving womb of the earth bids it go free into life
And to stimulant light, the sacred, for ever in motion,
   It trusts the delicate work of making the burgeoning leaves.
Simple the force asleep in the seed; an incipient model   15
   Lay, enclosed in itself, curled up there under the sheath,
Leaf and rootlet and bud, only half-formed with no colour;
   Thus the kernel sustains tranquil life in the dry,
Straining upward it swells, on gentle moisture relying,
   Quickly lifting itself from the encompassing night.   20
But the form remains in its first appearance still simple;
   And so the plants too show features denoting the child.
Straightaway a following thrust, risiiiing likewise, renews it,
   Piling up node upon node, always that first innate form.
Though not always the same one; for always leaves that come after 25
   Differ, as you can see, reproduce manifold,
More extended, more dented, more split into tips and with members
   Which before had been joined when in the organ below.
And thus it reaches at first the most specific perfection
   Which in many a kind moves and astonishes you.   30
Much serrated and ribbed, on gorged and swelling surface,
   Now the abundance of thrust seems to be endless and free.
Here though with hands overpowering nature reins back the force
   That shapes, and steers it smooth to make it more perfect still.
Moderate now it conducts the sap, and narrows the vessels,   35
   The form showing at once much more delicate effects.
Gradually the thrust recedes from the onpushing edges
   And the rib of the stalk takes on more fullness and girth.
Leafless now though and quick the stem more delicate rises
   And a marvel of form holds the observer enthralled.   40

Rings im Kreise stellet sich nun, gezählet und ohne
   Zahl, das kleinere Blatt neben dem ähnlichen hin.
Um die Achse gedrängt, entscheidet der bergende Kelch sich,
   Der zur höchsten Gestalt farbige Kronen entläßt.
Also prangt die Natur in hoher, voller Erscheinung,   45
   Und sie zeiget, gereiht, Glieder an Glieder gestuft.
Immer staunst du aufs neue, sobald sich am Stengel die Blume
   Über dem schlanken Gerüst wechselnder Blätter bewegt.
Aber die Herrlichkeit wird des neuen Schaffens Verkündung;
   Ja, das farbige Blatt fühlet die göttliche Hand,   50
Und zusammen zieht es sich schnell; die zärtesten Formen,
   Zwiefach streben sie vor, sich zu vereinen bestimmt.
Traulich stehen sie nun, die holden Paare, beisammen,
   Zahlreich ordnen sie sich um den geweihten Altar.
Hymen schwebet herbei, und herrliche Düfte, gewaltig,   55
   Strömen süßen Geruch, alles belebend, umher.
Nun vereinzelt schwellen sogleich unzählige Keime,
   Hold in den Mutterschoß schwellender Früchte gehüllt.
Und hier schließt die Natur den Ring der ewigen Kräfte;
   Doch ein neuer sogleich fasset den vorigen an,   60
Daß die Kette sich fort durch alle Zeiten verlänge
   Und das Ganze belebt, so wie das Einzelne, sei.
Wende nun, o Geliebte, den Blick zum bunten Gewimmel,
   Das verwirrend nicht mehr sich vor dem Geiste bewegt.
Jede Pflanze verkündet dir nun die ew'gen Gesetze,   65
   Jede Blume, sie spricht lauter und lauter mit dir.
Aber entzifferst du hier der Göttin heilige Lettern,
   Überall siehst du sie dann, auch in verändertem Zug.
Kriechend zaudre die Raupe, der Schmetterling eile geschäftig,
   Bildsam ändre der Mensch selbst die bestimmte Gestalt.   70
O, gedenke denn auch, wie aus dem Keim der Bekanntschaft
   Nach und nach in uns holde Gewohnheit entsproß,
Freundschaft sich mit Macht aus unserm Innern enthüllte,
   Und wie Amor zuletzt Blüten und Früchte gezeugt.
Denke, wie mannigfach bald die, bald jene Gestalten,   75
   Still entfaltend, Natur unsern Gefühlen geliehn!
Freue dich auch des heutigen Tags! Die heilige Liebe
   Strebt zu der höchsten Frucht gleicher Gesinnungen auf,
Gleicher Ansicht der Dinge, damit in harmonischem Anschaun
   Sich verbinde das Paar, finde die höhere Welt.   80

Forming a circle they take their place, all counted yet past all
   Counting, leaves much more small stand next to similar leaves.
Round the axis compressed the sheltering calyx develops
   And, for ultimate form, coloured corollas emits.
Nature thus comes to flaunt in full and highest appearance,   45
   Showing, ordered in steps, members on members arranged.
Always newly it stuns you as soon as the flower starts moving
   Over the varying leaves' scaffold built light round the stem.
But this great glory speaks to proclaim still newer creating;
   Yes, the bright coloured leaf senses divinity's hand   50
And it quickly draws itself in; most delicate forms now,
   Twinned they push themselves through, destined and made to unite.
Harmoniously they stand, the gracious couples, together,
   Numerously arranged all round the altar divine.
Hymen hovers above, and splendours of fragrance, compelling,   55
   Pour sweet odours around quickening all things with life.
Separated, numberless seeds at once begin swelling
   Wrapped in the swelling fruits' tenderly mothering womb.
And here nature completes the ring of perpetual forces;
   But a new one at once seizes the previous one   60
So that the chain carries on and through all ages continues
   Whereby the whole can become, like the particular, live.
Look again, O my dearest, and watch the colourful turmoil,
   Which confuses no more as in the mind's eye it moves.
Now every plant will proclaim to you the laws everlasting,   65
   Every flower will speak louder and louder to you.
If you decipher it here, the sacred script of the goddess,
   Everywhere it appears, even when altered in style.
The hesitant larva may crawl, the butterfly busily hurry,
   Malleable man himself transform his own given form.   70
O be mindful as well, how from the seed of acquaintance
   Bud by bud in us a sweetest accustoming sprang,
Friendship with such power emerged from deep down within us,
   And how Amor at last flowers and fruit has produced.
Think too how nature forms now this, now that way our feelings,   75
   Here too you can observe forms as they quietly unfold!
Also rejoice in this day! For love ever sacred aspires
   To produce in like minds fruit of the highest degree,
In a likeness of view so in harmonious vision
   Joined the pair may unite, rise to that high other world.   80

Weltseele

Verteilet euch nach allen Regionen
Von diesem heil'gen Schmaus!
Begeistert reißt euch durch die nächsten Zonen
Ins All und füllt es aus!

Schon schwebet ihr in ungemeßnen Fernen 5
Den sel'gen Göttertraum,
Und leuchtet neu, gesellig, unter Sternen
Im lichtbesäten Raum.

Dann treibt ihr euch, gewaltige Kometen,
Ins Weit' und Weitr' hinan. 10
Das Labyrinth der Sonnen und Planeten
Durchschneidet eure Bahn.

Ihr greifet rasch nach ungeformten Erden
Und wirket schöpf'risch jung,
Daß sie belebt und stets belebter werden 15
Im abgemeßnen Schwung.

Und kreisend führt ihr in bewegten Lüften
Den wandelbaren Flor,
Und schreibt dem Stein in allen seinen Grüften
Die festen Formen vor. 20

Nun alles sich mit göttlichem Erkühnen
Zu übertreffen strebt;
Das Wasser will, das unfruchtbare, grünen,
Und jedes Stäubchen lebt.

Und so verdrängt mit liebevollen Streiten 25
Der feuchten Qualme Nacht;
Nun glühen schon des Paradieses Weiten
In überbunter Pracht.

Wie regt sich bald, ein holdes Licht zu schauen,
Gestaltenreiche Schar, 30
Und ihr erstaunt auf den beglückten Auen
Nun als das erste Paar.

Und bald verlischt ein unbegrenztes Streben
Im sel'gen Wechselblick.
Und so empfangt mit Dank das schönste Leben 35
Vom All ins All zurück.

World Soul[7] (1798–1802)

Depart this feast of sacred dedication
And search all worlds about!
Rush through the universe in pure elation,
Enthuse and fill it out!

In blissful soaring through unfathomed distance   5
The dream of gods you dream,
With stars and seeding light in new existence
You join in space and gleam.

Then, mighty comets, thrusting through the notion
Of far and further space   10
You intersect the labyrinthine motion
That suns and planets pace.

You snatch and grasp for worlds not yet created
With youth's productive urge,
So that they live for ever animated   15
With every measured surge.

Through eddied airs you circle firmly guiding
The plant that changing grows,
You rule the stone in deepest caverns hiding
And stable forms impose.   20

Their nature to surpass with godlike power
Now all things boldly strive;
And water, barren, wants to green and flower,
Each speck of dust's alive.

Thus banish by your efforts, caring, steady,   25
The dank and murk of night;
Now Paradise in splendours glows already
Exuberantly bright.

How soon to see the grace of light life presses,
How hosts of forms are raised,   30
And now you stand on smiling fields it blesses
As earth's first pair amazed.

Soon impulse ebbs in joy's reciprocation,
In bliss of eye and soul.
And so receive with thanks life's consummation   35
In Wholeness from the Whole.

[*Natur und Kunst*]

Natur und Kunst, sie scheinen sich zu fliehen
Und haben sich, eh' man es denkt, gefunden;
Der Widerwille ist auch mir verschwunden,
Und beide scheinen gleich mich anzuziehen.

Es gilt wohl nur ein redliches Bemühen!   5
Und wenn wir erst in abgemeßnen Stunden
Mit Geist und Fleiß uns an die Kunst gebunden,
Mag frei Natur im Herzen wieder glühen.

So ist's mit aller Bildung auch beschaffen:
Vergebens werden ungebundne Geister   10
Nach der Vollendung reiner Höhe streben.

Wer Großes will, muß sich zusammenraffen;
In der Beschränkung zeigt sich erst der Meister,
Und das Gesetz nur kann uns Freiheit geben.

In goldnen Frühlingssonnenstunden

In goldnen Frühlingssonnenstunden
Lag ich gebunden
An dies Gesicht.
In holder Dunkelheit der Sinnen
Konnt' ich wohl diesen Traum beginnen,   5
Vollenden nicht.

Aus *Zum Neuen Jahr*

Zwischen dem Alten,
Zwischen dem Neuen,
Hier uns zu freuen
Schenkt uns das Glück,
Und das Vergangne   5
Heißt mit Vertrauen
Vorwärts zu schauen,
Schauen zurück.

*

[*Nature and Art*] (*1800*)

Though art and nature seem sore disunited
Yet each, before you think, to each is turning;
I too no longer sense discordant spurning,
By equal pulls seem equally excited.

An honest effort's bound to be requited!   5
If measured hours we dedicate to learning
And bind ourselves to art with zeal discerning
The heart may glow with nature new ignited.

So too all forming culture needs some tether:
Unbridled spirits end in vain disaster   10
Pursuing pure perfection's elevation.

Who wants great things must get himself together;
Constraint is where you show you are a master,
And only law is freedom's sure foundation.

When spring's gold sunshine hours enspelled me (*1800*)

When spring's gold sunshine hours enspelled me
This vision held me
In raptured mood.
In the senses' dark and fruitful teeming
I was able to start this dreaming,   5
But not conclude.

From *To the New Year* (*1801*)

Old Year is passing,
New Year is waiting,
We're celebrating
Good fortune today;
What's past finds its meaning   5
When trust is our tutor
In seeing the future
And the past's true assay.

*

Andere schauen
Denkende Falten   10
Über dem Alten
Traurig und scheu;
Aber uns leuchtet
Freundliche Treue;
Sehet, das Neue   15
Findet uns neu.

Dauer im Wechsel

Hielte diesen frühen Segen,
Ach, nur eine Stunde fest!
Aber vollen Blütenregen
Schüttelt schon der laue West.
Soll ich mich des Grünen freuen,   5
Dem ich Schatten erst verdankt?
Bald wird Sturm auch das zerstreuen,
Wenn es falb im Herbst geschwankt.

Willst du nach den Früchten greifen,
Eilig nimm dein Teil davon!   10
Diese fangen an zu reifen,
Und die andern keimen schon;
Gleich mit jedem Regengusse
Ändert sich dein holdes Tal,
Ach, und in demselben Flusse   15
Schwimmst du nicht zum zweitenmal.

Du nun selbst! Was felsenfeste
Sich vor dir hervorgetan,
Mauern siehst du, siehst Paläste
Stets mit andern Augen an.   20
Weggeschwunden ist die Lippe,
Die im Kusse sonst genas,
Jener Fuß, der an der Klippe
Sich mit Gemsenfreche maß.

Jene Hand, die gern und milde   25
Sich bewegte wohlzutun,
Das gegliederte Gebilde,
Alles ist ein andres nun.

Others see only
The Old Year shadowed,   10
Wrinkled and harrowed,
Sad fearful mood;
We though see shining
Friendship and trusting;
See, the New thrusting   15
Finds us renewed!

Lasting Change (1803)

Oh, if only springtime's blessing
Could be held for just one hour!
But the mild west wind is pressing
And already blossoms shower.
All this green, should I enjoy it,   5
Grateful for its recent shade?
Autumn's storms will soon destroy it
Once it's rocked the leaves that fade.

From the fruits your share ensuring
Grasp them quickly as you need!   10
These ones here begin maturing
And already others seed;
See your lovely valley quiver,
Altering instantly in rain;
Oh, and in the self-same river   15
you will never swim again.

And now you! Those things you reckoned
Firm as mountains in the skies,
Walls and palaces each second
You will see with other eyes.   20
Gone the lip which found in kisses
Healing in those former times,
And bold foot from precipices
Where the mountain goat still climbs.

And that hand, with warm devotion   25
Always opening good to do,
Membered living form in motion,
Now all that's some other too.

Und was sich an jener Stelle
Nun mit deinem Namen nennt,   30
Kam herbei wie eine Welle,
Und so eilt's zum Element.

Laß den Anfang mit dem Ende
Sich in e i n s zusammenziehn!
Schneller als die Gegenstände   35
Selber dich vorüberfliehn.
Danke, daß die Gunst der Musen
Unvergängliches verheißt,
Den Gehalt in deinem Busen
Und die Form in deinem Geist.   40

Was auch als Wahrheit oder fabel

Was auch als Wahrheit oder Fabel
In tausend Büchern dir erscheint,
Das alles ist ein Turm zu Babel,
Wenn es die Liebe nicht vereint.

And whatever all displaces –
That to which your name's now lent –   30
Came here like a wave that races
Onwards to the element.

Let the start and end so fusing
Join in One and unify!
Swifter than the things you're losing   35
You must let yourself go by!
Thank the Muses for bestowing
Favour of a lasting kind:
Import from your heart outflowing
And the form within your mind.   40

Whatever you think truth or fable (1805)

Whatever you think truth or fable
That in a thousand books you find
It all remains a Tower of Babel
Unless it is by love combined.

SONETTE

I

Mächtiges Überraschen

Ein Strom entrauscht umwölktem Felsensaale,
Dem Ozean sich eilig zu verbinden;
Was auch sich spiegeln mag von Grund zu Gründen,
Er wandelt unaufhaltsam fort zu Tale.

Dämonisch aber stürzt mit einem Male –   5
Ihr folgen Berg und Wald in Wirbelwinden –
Sich Oreas, Behagen dort zu finden,
Und hemmt den Lauf, begrenzt die weite Schale.

Die Welle sprüht und staunt zurück und weichet
Und schwillt bergan, sich immer selbst zu trinken;   10
Gehemmt ist nun zum Vater hin das Streben.

Sie schwankt und ruht, zum See zurückgedeichet;
Gestirne, spiegelnd sich, beschaun das Blinken
Des Wellenschlags am Fels, ein neues Leben.

II

Freundliches Begegnen

Im weiten Mantel bis ans Kinn verhüllet,
Ging ich den Felsenweg, den schroffen, grauen,
Hernieder dann zu winterhaften Auen,
Unruh'gen Sinns, zur nahen Flucht gewillet.

Auf einmal schien der neue Tag enthüllet: 5
Ein Mädchen kam, ein Himmel anzuschauen,
So musterhaft wie jene lieben Frauen
Der Dichterwelt. Mein Sehnen war gestillet.

Doch wandt' ich mich hinweg und ließ sie gehen
Und wickelte mich enger in die Falten,   10
Als wollt' ich trutzend in mir selbst erwarmen;

Und folgt' ihr doch. Sie stand. Da war's geschehen!
In meiner Hülle konnt' ich mich nicht halten,
Die warf ich weg, sie lag in meinen Armen.

SONNET CYCLE (*1807–8*)

I

Unexpected Overwhelming

From clouded rocky vaults a river gushes,
To join the distant ocean downwards racing:
Its course unchecked through mirrored valleys tracing,
Into the valley on and on it pushes.

But Oreas, daimonic, sudden rushes –   5
With cliff and forest too in whirlwinds chasing –
To seek contentment in that flow's embracing
And halts it, forms a vessel ringed with bushes.

The wave spurts foam and then retreats, astounded,
And drinks itself in swirl of backwards streaming;   10
The striving to the Father is abated.

It sways and rests, and as a lake is bounded;
The constellations, mirrored, watch the gleaming
As wave laps rock, as new life is created.

II

Friendly Meeting

Enveloped in my cloak, the serpentining
Track I traced that fell through mist and boulder
To wintering fields below and ever colder;
Escape was all my restless mind's inclining.

Then suddenly there was a new day shining: 5
A girl appeared; transported I behold her
Exemplary as poet's liege from older
And fabled times. It quieted my pining.

I let her pass and turned away, misguided,
More tightly wrapped myself in folds constraining   10
Like one whose scorn all other warmth replaces;

Yet followed her. She stopped. Then fate decided.
No longer in my cloak myself containing
I cast it off, she lay in my embraces.

III

Kurz und Gut

Sollt' ich mich denn so ganz an sie gewöhnen?
Das wäre mir zuletzt doch reine Plage.
Darum versuch' ich's gleich am heut'gen Tage
Und nahe nicht dem vielgewohnten Schönen.

Wie aber mag ich dich, mein Herz, versöhnen,   5
Daß ich im wicht'gen Fall dich nicht befrage?
Wohlan! Komm her! Wir äußern unsre Klage
In liebevollen, traurig heitern Tönen.

Siehst du, es geht! Des Dichters Wink gewärtig
Melodisch klingt die durchgespielte Leier,   10
Ein Liebesopfer traulich darzubringen.

Du denkst es kaum, und sieh: das Lied ist fertig;
Allein was nun? – Ich dächt', im ersten Feuer
Wir eilten hin, es vor ihr selbst zu singen.

IV

Das Mädchen Spricht

Du siehst so ernst, Geliebter! Deinem Bilde
Von Marmor hier möcht' ich dich wohl vergleichen;
Wie dieses gibst du mir kein Lebenszeichen;
Mit dir verglichen zeigt der Stein sich milde.

Der Feind verbirgt sich hinter seinem Schilde,   5
Der Freund soll offen seine Stirn uns reichen,
Ich suche dich, du suchst mir zu entweichen;
Doch halte stand wie dieses Kunstgebilde.

An wen von beiden soll ich nun mich wenden?
Sollt' ich von beiden Kälte leiden müssen,   10
Da dieses tot und du lebendig heißest?

Kurz, um der Worte mehr nicht zu verschwenden,
So will ich diesen Stein so lange küssen,
Bis eifersüchtig du mich ihm entreißest.

III

Enough

Should I with her completely be contented?
I'd finish up with only irritation.
That's why today I'll try some abnegation
And from her customed beauty be absented.

My heart, I did not ask if you assented;   5
For such grave fault what reconciliation?
So be it! Come! Our loving lamentation
In sounds serenely sad shall be presented.

You see, it works! We're half-anticipated,
The poet's muse already rhapsodises   10
On selfless love with melodies endearing.

You've hardly thought, and see, the song's created;
What now? – I think while this fresh fire surprises
We'll hurry off and sing it in her hearing.

IV

The Girl Speaks

You look so stern, my love! as here reflected
In this, your marble bust, that prompts comparing:
Like it you give no sign of life or caring,
Yet stone seems softer and the more affected.

The foe will take a shield to be protected,   5
The friend should have a frankly open bearing.
I seek you, you draw back as from a snaring;
Stand firm now, like this work that art perfected.

And now to which one should I look for favour?
Must I by both alike be treated coldly   10
When this is dead but you have life that warms you?

Enough, with idle talk I'll no more haver;
And so I'll kiss this marble statue boldly
Until you drag me off as envy storms you.

V

Wachstum

Als kleines, art'ges Kind nach Feld und Auen
Sprangst du mit mir so manchen Frühlingsmorgen.
'Für solch ein Töchterchen mit holden Sorgen
Möcht' ich als Vater segnend Häuser bauen!'

Und als du anfingst in die Welt zu schauen,   5
War deine Freude häusliches Besorgen.
'Solch eine Schwester! und ich wär' geborgen:
Wie könnt' ich ihr, ach! wie sie mir vertrauen!'

Nun kann den schönen Wachstum nichts beschränken;
Ich fühl' im Herzen heißes Liebetoben.   10
Umfass' ich sie, die Schmerzen zu beschwicht'gen?

Doch ach! nun muß ich dich als Fürstin denken:
Du stehst so schroff vor mir emporgehoben;
Ich beuge mich vor deinem Blick, dem flücht'gen.

VI

Reisezehrung

Entwöhnen sollt' ich mich vom Glanz der Blicke,
Mein Leben sollten sie nicht mehr verschönen.
Was man Geschick nennt, läßt sich nicht versöhnen;
Ich weiß es wohl und trat bestürzt zurücke.

Nun wußt' ich auch von keinem weitern Glücke;   5
Gleich fing ich an von diesen und von jenen
Notwend'gen Dingen sonst mich zu entwöhnen:
Notwendig schien mir nichts als ihre Blicke.

Des Weines Glut, den Vielgenuß der Speisen,
Bequemlichkeit und Schlaf und sonst'ge Gaben,   10
Gesellschaft wies ich weg, daß wenig bliebe.

So kann ich ruhig durch die Welt nun reisen:
Was ich bedarf, ist überall zu haben,
Und Unentbehrlich's bring' ich mit – die Liebe.

V

Growth

With you, a little skipping child, I'd wander
With springtime dawn the fields and meadows sharing.
'For such a daughter I'd be quite unsparing,
To build her houses all my wealth I'd squander!'

When later you on life began to ponder   5
Your pleasure was for household tasks preparing.
'With such a sister! she would be so caring:
In our confiding each would be the fonder!'

Now for that lovely growth there's no confining;
My heart endures love's raging conflagration.   10
Should I embrace her, from such pains to ease me?

Alas! as for a princess now I'm pining:
Abruptly, now you're high above my station;
I bow before your glance that hardly sees me.

VI

Provisions

I had to leave those looks from her I needed,
That radiance and my life's illumination.
What we call fate brooks no accommodation;
So I withdrew and to fate's shock conceded.

All other happiness was superseded;   5
At once I exercised renunciation,
Of this and that need practised deprivation:
Those looks from her alone seemed all I needed.

The warmth of wine, food's relish, gifts unnumbered,
Companions, comforts, sleep, all now redundant!   10
I cast them off, the minimum retaining.

At ease I walk the world now, unencumbered:
To meet my need the world has stuff abundant;
I carry what's essential – love's sustaining.

VII

Abschied

War unersättlich nach viel tausend Küssen,
Und mußt’ mit Einem Kuß am Ende scheiden.
Nach herber Trennung tiefempfundnem Leiden
War mir das Ufer, dem ich mich entrissen,

Mit Wohnungen, mit Bergen, Hügeln, Flüssen,   5
Solang ich’s deutlich sah, ein Schatz der Freuden;
Zuletzt im Blauen blieb ein Augenweiden
An fernentwichnen lichten Finsternissen.

Und endlich, als das Meer den Blick umgrenzte,
Fiel mir zurück ins Herz mein heiß Verlangen;   10
Ich suchte meine Verlornes gar verdrossen.

Da war es gleich, als ob der Himmel glänzte;
Mir schien, als wäre nichts mir, nichts entgangen,
Als hätt’ ich alles, was ich je genossen.

VIII

Die Liebende Schreibt

Ein Blick von deinen Augen in die meinen,
Ein Kuß von deinem Mund auf meinem Munde,
Wer davon hat, wie ich, gewisse Kunde,
Mag dem was andres wohl erfreulich scheinen?

Entfernt von dir, entfremdet von den Meinen,   5
Führ’ ich stets die Gedanken in die Runde,
Und immer treffen sie auf jene Stunde,
Die einzige: da fang’ ich an zu weinen.

Die Träne trocknet wieder unversehens;
Er liebt ja, denk’ ich, her in diese Stille,   10
Und solltest du nicht in die Ferne reichen?

Vernimm das Lispeln dieses Liebewehens!
Mein einzig Glück auf Erden ist dein Wille,
Dein freundlicher zu mir; gib mir ein Zeichen!

VII

Parting

From many thousand kisses still unsated
There came with one last kiss the separation.
And after parting's bitter immolation
I pulled off from the shore while pain abated

As houses, mountains, streams I contemplated,   5
To see them was a treasured compensation;
Then eye's delight, the distant indication
Of blue horizons darkly animated.

Until my heart was scorched again by yearning,
To see at last the open sea before me;   10
I searched for all I'd lost with grim obsession.

Then suddenly it seemed the heavens were burning;
I'd nothing lost, and wholly to restore me
All previous joys returned as my possession.

VIII

His Love Writes

One look from yours to mine your love imparted,
Your mouth on mine one single kiss bestowing;
For such as me, and after such a knowing,
Can any other happiness be charted?

So far from you, from all my near ones parted,   5
I watch my thoughts that circle to-and froing
Forever to that single hour flowing,
The only one: and now my tears have started.

But unexpectedly my tears are ending;
His love, I think, breaks through my isolation   10
So should you not reach him with words unspoken?

Hear now this whispered breath of love I'm sending!
My only fortune and my consolation
Is your fond will; oh send to me some token!

IX

Die Liebende Abermals

Warum ich wieder zum Papier mich wende?
Das mußt du, Liebster, so bestimmt nicht fragen:
Denn eigentlich hab' ich dir nichts zu sagen;
Doch kommt's zuletzt in deine lieben Hände.

Weil ich nicht kommen kann, soll, was ich sende,   5
Mein ungeteiltes Herz hinübertragen
Mit Wonnen, Hoffnungen, Entzücken, Plagen:
Das alles hat nicht Anfang, hat nicht Ende.

Ich mag vom heut'gen Tag dir nichts vertrauen,
Wie sich im Sinnen, Wünschen, Wähnen, Wollen   10
Mein treues Herz zu dir hinüberwendet:

So stand ich einst vor dir, dich anzuschauen,
Und sagte nichts. Was hätt' ich sagen sollen?
Mein ganzes Wesen war in sich vollendet.

X

Sie kann nicht Enden

Wenn ich nun gleich das weiße Blatt dir schickte,
Anstatt daß ich's mit Lettern erst beschreibe,
Ausfülltest du's vielleicht zum Zeitvertreibe
Und sendetest's an mich, die Hochbeglückte.

Wenn ich den blauen Umschlag dann erblickte;   5
Neugierig schnell, wie es geziemt dem Weibe,
Riss' ich ihn auf, daß nichts verborgen bleibe;
Da läs' ich, was mich mündlich sonst entzückte:

'Lieb Kind! Mein artig Herz! Mein einzig Wesen!'
Wie du so freundlich meine Sehnsucht stilltest   10
Mit süßem Wort und mich so ganz verwöhntest.

Sogar dein Lispeln glaubt' ich auch zu lesen,
Womit du liebend meine Seele fülltest
Und mich auf ewig vor mir selbst verschöntest.

IX

His Love Writes Again

Another note, and what am I intending?
That point, my love, you mustn't want decided:
For though there's nothing new to be confided
This note you'll hold in hands all compehending.

As I can't come this paper that I'm sending   5
Conveys to you my whole heart undivided,
By joys and hopes, delights and torments guided:
All that has no beginning, has no ending.

I can't tell of my day, how I adore you,
My sensing, wishing, dreams, and what I've wanted,   10
All day my faithful heart to you directed:

Once, just to look at you, I stood before you
And said no word. And what would words have counted?
I knew then all my being was perfected.

X

She Cannot End

If I were now this empty white sheet sending
Without first covering it with any writing
Perhaps you'd find to write on it inviting
And send it me whose joys you make unending.

As woman will, impulsively dependent,   5
I'd tear the envelope, be so excited
To know what's hidden and I'd be delighted
To read, as you once said them, words transcendent:

'Dear child! My sweetest heart! My only being!'
So you would spoil me with sweet words adoring   10
And still my yearning when we were together.

Your murmuring as well I'd think I'm seeing
As when you filled my soul, your love outpouring,
In me my beauty imaging for ever.

XI

Nemesis

Wenn durch das Volk die grimme Seuche wütet,
Soll man vorsichtig die Gesellschaft lassen.
Auch hab' ich oft mit Zaudern und Verpassen
Vor manchen Influenzen mich gehütet.

Und obgleich Amor öfters mich begütet,   5
Mocht' ich zuletzt mich nicht mit ihm befassen.
So ging mir's auch mit jenen Lacrimassen,
Als vier-und dreifach reimend sie gebrütet.

Nun aber folgt die Strafe dem Verächter,
Als wenn die Schlangenfackel der Erinnen   10
Von Berg zu Tal, von Land zu Meer ihn triebe.

Ich höre wohl der Genien Gelächter;
Doch trennet mich von jeglichem Besinnen
Sonettenwut und Raserei der Liebe.

XII

Christgeschenk

Mein süßes Liebchen! Hier in Schachtelwänden
Gar mannigfalt geformte Süßigkeiten.
Die Früchte sind es heil'ger Weihnachtszeiten,
Gebackne nur, den Kindern auszuspenden!

Dir möcht' ich dann mit süßem Redewenden   5
Poetisch Zuckerbrot zum Fest bereiten;
Allein was soll's mit solchen Eitelkeiten?
Weg den Versuch, mit Schmeichelei zu blenden!

Doch gibt es noch ein Süßes, das vom Innern
Zum Innern spricht, genießbar in der Ferne,   10
Das kann nur bis zu dir hinüberwehen.

Und fühlst du dann ein freundliches Erinnern,
Als blinkten froh dir wohlbekannte Sterne,
Wirst du die kleinste Gabe nicht verschmähen.

XI

Nemesis

When all the nation's by fierce plague infected
It's best to stay in prudent isolation.
And by omission and by hesitation
From influences I have stayed protected.

By Amor often favoured and selected   5
I found with him no lasting occupation.
And so it was with all that 'Lachrymation'[8]
When three- and fourfold rhyming was expected.

But he who scorns finds punishment comes after,
As by the Furies' snaking torch tormented   10
From hill to vale, from land to sea he's driven.

Yet though I hear the Spirits' scornful laughter
It does not sober me since I'm demented,
By sonnet mania and love's madness riven.

XII

Christmas Present

My sweetest love! Here for your Christmas platter
Accept the varied sweets this carton's bearing.
They're fruits we bake for children, so declaring
That Christmas is a sweet and holy matter!

Poetic sweetmeats in rhetoric chatter,   5
This festival for you I've been preparing;
Yet for such vanities as these, who's caring?
Away with this attempt to blind and flatter!

But from within and inwardly to meet you,
Erasing distance, come sweet consolations   10
That only in the air can be detected.

If you then feel dear memories that greet you
As from the shine of well-known constellations
I trust these smaller gifts won't be rejected.

XIII

Warnung

Am Jüngsten Tag, wenn die Posaunen schallen,
Und alles aus ist mit dem Erdeleben,
Sind wir verpflichtet, Rechenschaft zu geben
Von jedem Wort, das unnütz uns entfallen.

Wie wird's nun werden mit den Worten allen,   5
In welchen ich so liebevoll mein Streben
Um deine Gunst dir an den Tag gegeben,
Wenn diese bloß an deinem Ohr verhallen?

Darum bedenk', o Liebchen, dein Gewissen,
Bedenk' im Ernst, wie lange du gezaudert,   10
Daß nicht der Welt solch Leiden widerfahre.

Werd' ich berechnen und entschuld'gen müssen,
Was alles unnütz ich vor dir geplaudert,
So wird der Jüngste Tag zum vollen Jahre.

XIV

Die Zweifelnden:

Ihr liebt, und schreibt Sonette! Weh der Grille!
Die Kraft des Herzens, sich zu offenbaren,
Soll Reime suchen, sie zusammenpaaren;
Ihr Kinder, glaubt: ohnmächtig bleibt der Wille.

Ganz ungebunden spricht des Herzens Fülle   5
Sich kaum noch aus: sie mag sich gern bewahren;
Dann Stürmen gleich durch alle Saiten fahren;
Dann wieder senken sich zu Nacht und Stille.

Was quält ihr euch und uns, auf jähem Stege
Nur Schritt vor Schritt den läst'gen Stein zu wälzen,   10
Der rückwärts lastet, immer neu zu mühen?

Die Liebenden:

Im Gegenteil, wir sind auf rechtem Wege!
Das Allerstarrste freudig aufzuschmelzen,
Muß Liebesfeuer allgewaltig glühen.

XIII

Warning

On that Last Day when loud the trumpet's sounded
And this our earthly life must be surrendered,
Account must then for every word be rendered
Which uselessly my vanity compounded.

Then by my many words shall I be foundered   5
Which striving for your grace in me engendered
And I so lovingly to you have tendered?
What then, if all my words should prove ungrounded?

Consider then what conscience now refuses,
Consider, dearest, how you've hesitated,   10
That by such pain our world be not offended.

If I must calculate and make excuses
For all the words on you I've dissipated
That Last Day to a year must be extended.

XIV

Doubters:

You love, and so write sonnets! All's pretended!
You think that coupling rhymes in such composing
Can sate the heart that craves the heart's disclosing;
Believe us, dears, you'll find your will's suspended.

Not even words whose flow is never ended   5
Can tell heart's plenitude: it likes reposing;
Then storm-like all the strings and stops disposing;
Then being again to still of night surrendered.

Why torture then yourselves and us who read you
To push the stone uphill in steps so tiring   10
Whilst back it rolls and makes the struggle harder?

Lovers:

Our way is right, so don't let that mislead you!
To melt the hardest stuff needs only firing
By all-consuming love's commanding ardour.

XV

Mädchen:

Ich zweifle doch am Ernst verschränkter Zeilen!
Zwar lausch' ich gern bei deinen Silbespielen;
Allein mir scheint, was Herzen redlich fühlen,
Mein süßer Freund, das soll man nicht befeilen.

Der Dichter pflegt, um nicht zu langeweilen,   5
Sein Innerstes von Grund aus umzuwühlen;
Doch seine Wunden weiß er auszukühlen,
Mit Zauberwort die tiefsten auszuheilen.

Dichter:

Schau, Liebchen, hin: Wie geht's dem Feuerwerker?
Drauf ausgelernt, wie man nach Maßen wettert,   10
Irrgänglich-klug miniert er seine Grüfte;

Allein die Macht des Elements ist stärker,
Und eh' er sich's versieht, geht er zerschmettert
Mit allen seinen Künsten in die Lüfte.

XVI

Epoche

Mit Flammenschrift war innigst eingeschrieben
Petrarcas Brust vor allen andern Tagen
Karfreitag. Eben so, ich darf's wohl sagen,
Ist mir Advent von Achtzehnhundertsieben.

Ich fing nicht an, ich fuhr nur fort zu lieben   5
Sie, die ich früh im Herzen schon getragen,
Dann wieder weislich aus dem Sinn geschlagen,
Der ich nun wieder bin ans Herz getrieben.

Petrarcas Liebe, die unendlich hohe,
War leider unbelohnt und gar zu traurig,   10
Ein Herzensweh, ein ewiger Karfreitag;

Doch stets erscheine, fort und fort, die frohe,
Süß, unter Palmenjubel, wonneschaurig,
Der Herrin Ankunft mir, ein ew'ger Maitag.

XV
Girl:

I doubt the worth of lines all interlacing!
Agreed, I find your wordplay's most appealing;
But surely what our hearts are truly feeling
Should not, my sweet, be wrought in bevelled casing.

The poet delves, when tedious themes replacing,   5
To churn his substance inside out revealing;
But for his wounds he knows a cooling healing,
The spell of words, his deepest scars effacing.

Poet:

But look, my dear, the sapper: how's his calling?
His training's to discharge a measured thunder,   10
The skill with which he drives his shafts amazes.

However, elemental power's appalling,
And suddenly with all his craft asunder
He's blown into the air and gone to blazes.

XVI

Epoch

In Petrarch's heart Good Friday's conflagration
Inscribed a testament forever burning.
So Advent was my own time's overturning
In Eighteen Seven, my year of exaltation.

It was no start, just love's continuation,   5
For her my heart much earlier was yearning
Till later on it turned to prudent spurning,
And now her heart's my lasting inclination.

Yet Petrarch's love, though infinite its soaring,
Was really sad and sadly unrewarded,   10
Eternally Good Friday's heart in mourning.

But let my lady come, with bliss outpouring,
Let gladly palms triumphant be accorded,
So on and on eternal Mayday dawning.

XVII

Scharade

Zwei Worte sind es, kurz, bequem zu sagen,
Die wir so oft mit holder Freude nennen,
Doch keineswegs die Dinge deutlich kennen,
Wovon sie eigentlich den Stempel tragen.

Es tut gar wohl in jung- und alten Tagen,   5
Eins an dem andern kecklich zu verbrennen;
Und kann man sie vereint zusammen nennen,
So drückt man aus ein seliges Behagen.

Nun aber such' ich ihnen zu gefallen
Und bitte, mit sich selbst mich zu beglücken;   10
Ich hoffe still, doch hoff' ich's zu erlangen:

Als Namen der Geliebten sie zu lallen,
In Einem Bild sie beide zu erblicken,
In Einem Wesen beide zu umfangen.

XVII

Charade⁹

Just two short words, and easy their expression,
How often with pure joy they've been recited
Although the seals are never clearly sighted
That stamp on them their meaning's true impression.

The days of youth and age we like to freshen   5
By boldly getting each by each ignited;
And if in one name they can be united
They sound like our well-being's glad confession.

But now I look for them in play that pleases
And hope their pleasure's into mine projected;   10
And silently I hope I'll soon be seeing:

In them my own love's name in mask that teases,
ONE image where they both can be detected
And I can both embrace in that ONE being.

Wär nicht das Auge sonnenhaft

Wär nicht das Auge sonnenhaft,
Die Sonne könnt' es nie erblicken;
Läg' nicht in uns des Gottes eigne Kraft,
Wie könnt' uns Göttliches entzücken?

Das Tagebuch

—*aliam tenui, sed iam quum gaudia adirem,*
Admonuit dominae deseruitque Venus.

Wir hören's oft und glauben's wohl am Ende:
Das Menschenherz sei ewig unergründlich,
Und wie man auch sich hin und wider wende,
So sei der Christe wie der Heide sündlich.
Das Beste bleibt, wir geben uns die Hände
Und nehmen's mit der Lehre nicht empfindlich;
Denn zeigt sich auch ein Dämon, uns versuchend,
So waltet was, gerettet ist die Tugend.

Von meiner Trauten lange Zeit entfernet,
Wie's öfters geht, nach irdischem Gewinne,
Und was ich auch gewonnen und gelernet,
So hatt ich doch nur immer Sie im Sinne;
Und wie zu Nacht der Himmel erst sich sternet,
Erinnrung uns umleuchtet ferner Minne:
So ward im Federzug des Tags Ereignis
Mit süßen Worten ihr ein freundlich Gleichnis.

Ich eilte nun zurück. Zerbrochen sollte
Mein Wagen mich noch eine Nacht verspäten;
Schon dacht ich mich, wie ich zu Hause rollte,
Allein da war Geduld und Werk vonnöten.
Und wie ich auch mit Schmied und Wagner tollte,
Sie hämmerten, verschmähten viel zu reden.
Ein jedes Handwerk hat nun seine Schnurren.
Was blieb mir nun? Zu weilen und zu murren.

Unless the eye had sunlike parts (1810)

Unless the eye had sunlike parts
It could not see the sun and sight us;
Unless the god's own power were in our hearts
How could what is divine delight us?

The Diary (1810)

I had another woman in my arms, but when
I was about to enjoy her, Venus called to mind my lady
and left me in the lurch.[10]

We hear it said and in the end believe it:
The human heart's unfathomable for ever,
And Christians, heathens, though they can't conceive it
Are all in sinful nature one together.
It's best that we shake hands on that and leave it,   5
That we don't chafe ourselves on doctrine's tether;
For though some spirit brings us in temptation
Some power still guards our virtue and salvation.

For long from my own darling separated,
As often happens, on some business dealing,   10
I earned and learned, was wined and dined and feted,
But I kept only her in thought and feeling:
It's night when sky by stars is penetrated
And far love grows in memory's unsealing,
And that's when I would pen to her my greeting,   15
In loving words each day's events repeating.

So now I hurried back. My carriage failed me,
It broke, and all my thoughts of home receded
By one more night, and such a rage assailed me
When work and patience were the things I needed.   20
The smith and wheelwright worked, no words availed me,
They held their tongue, my fury went unheeded.
Each craft has got its foibles, fads and fumble.
What then my role? None left but wait and grumble.

So stand ich nun. Der Stern des nächsten Schildes
Berief mich hin, die Wohnung schien erträglich.
Ein Mädchen kam, des seltensten Gebildes,
Das Licht erleuchtend. Mir ward gleich behäglich.
Hausflur und Treppe sah ich als ein Mildes,
Die Zimmerchen erfreuten mich unsäglich.
Den sündigen Menschen der im Freien schwebet –
Die Schönheit spinnt, sie ist's die ihn umwebet.

Nun setzt ich mich zu meiner Tasch und Briefen
Und meines Tagebuchs Genauigkeiten,
Um so wie sonst, wenn alle Menschen schliefen,
Mir und der Trauten Freude zu bereiten;
Doch weiß ich nicht, die Tintenworte liefen
Nicht so wie sonst in alle Kleinigkeiten:
Das Mädchen kam, des Abendessens Bürde
Verteilte sie gewandt mit Gruß und Würde.

Sie geht und kommt; ich spreche, sie erwidert;
Mit jedem Wort erscheint sie mir geschmückter.
Und wie sie leicht mir nun das Huhn zergliedert,
Bewegend Hand und Arm, geschickt, geschickter –
Was auch das tolle Zeug in uns befiedert –   45
Genug ich bin verworrner, bin verrückter,
Den Stuhl umwerfend spring ich auf und fasse
Das schöne Kind; sie lispelt: 'Lasse, lasse!

Die Muhme drunten lauscht, ein alter Drache;
Sie zählt bedächtig des Geschäfts Minute;   50
Sie denkt sich unten, was ich oben mache,
Bei jedem Zögern schwenkt sie frisch die Rute.
Doch schließe deine Türe nicht und wache,
So kommt die Mitternacht uns wohl zu Gute.'
Rasch meinem Arm entwindet sie die Glieder,   55
Und eilet fort und kommt nur dienend wieder;

Doch blickend auch! So daß aus jedem Blicke
Sich himmlisches Versprechen mir entfaltet.
Den stillen Seufzer drängt sie nicht zurücke,
Der ihren Busen herrlicher gestaltet.   60
Ich sehe, daß am Ohr, um Hals und G'nicke
Der flüchtgen Röte Liebesblüte waltet,
Und da sie nichts zu leisten weiter findet,
Geht sie und zögert, sieht sich um, verschwindet.

So there I was. The Star Inn's sign invited,   25
It really seemed not bad accommodation.
A girl, whose form superlative I sighted,
Brought light. I felt a cosy warm sensation.
By pleasant hall and stairs I was delighted,
By little rooms beyond all expectation.   30
When sinful man soars free how that refreshes –
Then beauty spins and takes him in her meshes.

And then I took the diary I'd been keeping
To please my darling with the usual letter
I loved to write her when the world was sleeping,   35
For then, alone with her, my words flowed better;
But somehow now my words were only creeping
As though my pen was troubled by some fetter:
The girl arrived and laid my supper-table
With courteous greetings, dignified and able.   40

She comes and goes. I speak, she speaks politely;
She seems more fair with every word she answers.
And as she carves my chicken, deft and lightly,
The grace of moving hand and arm entrances –
The stuff that makes the nonsense in us sprightly –   45
Enough, I'm lost, I'm mad, all reels and dances,
I leap up, chair knocked down, some force impels me
To grasp her: 'Don't, please don't' her whisper tells me;

'My aunt's downstairs, a dragon old and vicious,
She counts each minute, soon she'll be complaining;   50
When I'm up here she thinks and grows suspicious,
Each time I'm late I get another caning.
Don't lock your door, keep watch, and be judicious
Till midnight, then we'll both need no restraining.'
She struggles free and hurries out, all harassed;   55
Then later back, she serves me, unembarrassed

But with such looks! So that each look confesses,
Such heavenly promises each one proposes,
There's not one quiet sigh that she represses,
Each stirs her bosom, rounds it and discloses.   60
I see on ear, on neck, in nape's recesses
Love's blossom in the fleeting tint of roses.
She sees no more to do, looks round, half-hearted,
One hesitation more and she's departed.

Der Mitternacht gehören Haus und Straßen,   65
Mir ist ein weites Lager aufgebreitet,
Wovon den kleinsten Teil mir anzumaßen
Die Liebe rät, die alles wohl bereitet;
Ich zaudre noch, die Kerzen auszublasen,
Nun hör ich sie, wie leise sie auch gleitet,   70
Mit gierigem Blick die Hochgestalt umschweif ich,
Sie senkt sich her, die Wohlgestalt ergreif ich.

Sie macht sich los: 'Vergönne, daß ich rede,
Damit ich dir nicht völlig fremd gehöre.
Der Schein ist wider mich, sonst war ich blöde,   75
Stets gegen Männer setzt ich mich zur Wehre.
Mich nennt die Stadt, mich nennt die Gegend spröde;
Nun aber weiß ich, wie das Herz sich kehre:
Du bist mein Sieger, laß dich's nicht verdrießen,
Ich sah, ich liebte, schwur dich zu genießen.   80

Du hast mich rein, und wenn ich's besser wüßte,
So gäb ich's dir, ich tue was ich sage.'
So schließt sie mich an ihre süßen Brüste,
Als ob ihr nur an meiner Brust behage.
Und wie ich Mund und Aug und Stirne küßte,   85
So war ich doch in wunderbarer Lage:
Denn der so hitzig sonst den Meister spielet,
Weicht schülerhaft zurück und abgekühlet.

Ihr scheint ein süßes Wort, ein Kuß zu gnügen,
Als wär es alles was ihr Herz begehrte.   90
Wie keusch sie mir, mit liebevollem Fügen,
Des süßen Körpers Fülleform gewährte!
Entzückt und froh in allen ihren Zügen
Und ruhig dann, als wenn sie nichts entbehrte.
So ruh ich auch, gefällig sie beschauend,   95
Noch auf den Meister hoffend und vertrauend.

Doch als ich länger mein Geschick bedachte,
Von tausend Flüchen mir die Seele kochte,
Mich selbst verwünschend, grinsend mich belachte,
Nichts besser ward, wie ich auch zaudern mochte,   100
Da lag sie schlafend, schöner als sie wachte;
Die Lichter dämmerten mit langem Dochte.
Der Tages-Arbeit, jugendlicher Mühe
Gesellt sich gern der Schlaf und nie zu frühe.

In house and streets now midnight's peace is flowing; 65
Although for me a wide bed is provided
Love prompts, as ever good advice bestowing,
So mine's the smallest portion I've decided.
I hesitate then leave the candles glowing,
I hear her, though so quietly she's glided, 70
My passioned eyes explore her form exalted,
She lies down close, I clasp her form unfaulted.

She frees herself: 'First hear my explanation,
Then take me knowing all, no false pretences.
It doesn't look so, but my past relation 75
To men was timid, I was all defences.
Round here I have a prudish reputation;
My heart's now changed, you've brought me to my senses:
You've conquered me, so don't let it annoy you
That I saw, I loved, and swore that I'd enjoy you. 80

You take me pure, and were it in my power
I'd give you more if I knew more what pleases.'
Her sweet breasts press my breast, as though this hour
With me for her was all of all that eases. 85
On mouth and eyes and brow my kisses shower,
Then fate devised the oddest of his teases:
For he who's used to play the heated Master
As schoolboys do draws back and cools off faster.

It seems that tender words and soft caresses
Fulfil her heart from love so long absented. 90
Her body's sweet abundance chasteness blesses
And all to me she lovingly consented!
Such joyfulness and rapture she expresses
And then she rests as if she were contented.
I rested too, my fond gaze on her figure, 95
My hope and trust still with the Master's vigour.

I pondered my misfortune ill-encumbered,
In all my seething soul dark spirits snickered
And mocked, with curses, grins and jeers unnumbered,
And as I dithered, on and on they bickered 100
While she, more fair than when awake, just slumbered
As, lower now, the wavering candles flickered.
To youth that sweats and toils in daily labour
Sweet sleep comes easy as a welcome neighbour.

So lag sie himmlisch an bequemer Stelle,   105
Als wenn das Lager ihr allein gehörte,
Und an die Wand gedrückt, gequetscht zur Hölle,
Ohnmächtig jener, dem sie nichts verwehrte.
Vom Schlangenbisse fällt zunächst der Quelle
Ein Wandrer so, den schon der Durst verzehrte.   110
Sie atmet lieblich holdem Traum entgegen;
Er hält den Atem, sie nicht aufzuregen.

Gefaßt bei dem, was ihm noch nie begegnet,
Spricht er zu sich: So mußt du doch erfahren,
Warum der Bräutigam sich kreuzt und segnet,   115
Vor Nestelknüpfen scheu sich zu bewahren.
Weit lieber da, wo's Hellebarden regnet,
Als hier im Schimpf! So war es nicht vor Jahren,
Als deine Herrin dir zum ersten Male
Vors Auge trat im prachterhellten Saale.   120

Da quoll dein Herz, da quollen deine Sinnen,
So daß der ganze Mensch entzückt sich regte.
Zum raschen Tanze trugst du sie von hinnen,
Die kaum der Arm und schon der Busen hegte,
Als wolltest du dir selbst sie abgewinnen;   125
Vervielfacht war, was sich für sie bewegte:
Verstand und Witz und alle Lebensgeister
Und rascher als die andern jener Meister.

So immerfort wuchs Neigung und Begierde,
Brautleute wurden wir im frühen Jahre,   130
Sie selbst des Maien schönste Blum und Zierde;
Wie wuchs die Kraft zur Lust im jungen Paare!
Und als ich endlich sie zur Kirche führte,
Gesteh ich's nur, vor Priester und Altare,
Vor deinem Jammerkreuz, blutrünstger Christe,   135
Verzeih mir's Gott, es regte sich der Iste.

Und ihr, der Brautnacht reiche Bettgehänge,
Ihr Pfühle, die ihr euch so breit erstrecktet,
Ihr Teppiche, die Lieb und Lustgedränge
Mit euren seidnen Fittichen bedecktet!   140
Ihr Käfigvögel, die durch Zwitscher-Sänge
Zu neuer Lust und nie zu früh erwecktet!
Ihr kanntet uns, von euerm Schutz umfriedet,
Teilnehmend sie, mich immer unermüdet.

In comfort thus she lay like heaven's daughter 105
As if all hers the bed where she was lying,
And feeble, squashed against the wall's rough mortar,
The one to whom she nothing was denying.
Thus snakebite kills, just when he's reached the water,
The traveller of thirst already dying. 110
She dreams a dream in her own gracious making;
He holds his breath lest she have stir or waking.

He tells himself, this first time he's found failing:
You too now know why, fearing they'll be haltered,
Those bridegrooms cross themselves, in spirit quailing 115
Lest they by baleful knots be snared and faulted.
Far best the battlefield and bullets hailing
Than here disgraced! Since long ago you've altered
Since first, in blazing pomp of lights surrounded,
You saw your lady-liege and were astounded. 120

Your heart and senses surged and pricked and heated,
The whole man all ecstatically excited.
You rushed her off to dance, you'd scarcely greeted,
To hold at once as all of you delighted,
As though you with yourself for her competed; 125
Your powers multiplied that she ignited:
Your mind, wit, vital spirits, quickened faster,
And of them all the quickest was that Master.

Desire and inclination grew, compelling,
And early in the spring our troth was plighted, 130
Herself the fairest flowers of May excelling;
An eager pair, young appetites unblighted!
And when at last we wed – the truth needs telling –
Before the altar where we were united,
Before your anguished cross where you were martyred, 135
Dear Lord forgive me, That One stirred and started.[11]

You sumptuous bed, you pillows broad, that bore us
That bridal night when we became each other's,
You tapestries that, when urgent love would soar us
In passioned joys, would hide us in silk covers! 140
You cage-birds, never soon enough your chorus
That woke us to renew the zest of lovers!
You knew us well, at ease in your safe tending,
Her taking her fond part, me never ending.

Und wie wir oft sodann im Raub genossen   145
Nach Buhlenart des Ehstands heilige Rechte,
Von reifer Saat umwogt, von Rohr umschlossen,
An manchem Unort, wo ich's mich erfrechte,
Wir waren augenblicklich, unverdrossen
Und wiederholt bedient vom braven Knechte!   150
Verfluchter Knecht, wie unerwecklich liegst du!
Und deinen Herrn ums schönste Glück betriegst du!

Doch Meister Iste hat nun seine Grillen
Und läßt sich nicht befehlen noch verachten,
Auf einmal ist er da, und ganz im stillen   155
Erhebt er sich zu allen seinen Prachten;
So steht es nun dem Wandrer ganz zu Willen,
Nicht lechzend mehr am Quell zu übernachten.
Er neigt sich hin, er will die Schläferin küssen,
Allein er stockt, er fühlt sich weggerissen.   160

Wer hat zur Kraft ihn wieder aufgestählet,
Als jenes Bild, das ihm auf ewig teuer,
Mit dem er sich in Jugendlust vermählet?
Dort leuchtet her ein frisch erquicklich Feuer,
Und wie er erst in Ohnmacht sich gequälet,   165
So wird nun hier dem Starken nicht geheuer;
Er schaudert weg, vorsichtig, leise, leise
Entzieht er sich dem holden Zauberkreise,

Sitzt, schreibt: 'Ich nahte mich der heimischen Pforte,
Entfernen wollten mich die letzten Stunden,   170
Da hab ich nun, am sonderbarsten Orte,
Mein treues Herz aufs neue dir verbunden.
Zum Schlusse findest du geheime Worte:
Die Krankheit erst bewähret den Gesunden.
Dies Büchlein soll dir manches Gute zeigen,   175
Das Beste nur muß ich zuletzt verschweigen.'

Da kräht der Hahn. Das Mädchen schnell entwindet
Der Decke sich und wirft sich rasch ins Mieder.
Und da sie sich so seltsam wiederfindet,
So stutzt sie, blickt und schlägt die Augen nieder;   180
Und da sie ihm zum letzten Mal verschwindet,
Im Auge bleiben ihm die schönen Glieder:
Das Posthorn tönt, er wirft sich in den Wagen
Und läßt getrost sich zu der Liebsten tragen.

And often later, when we'd be securing   145
In secret holy wedlock's rights so gracious,
In sedge's screen, in waves of corn maturing,
And less fit places where I'd grow audacious,
We got such instant service reassuring
From that fine servant, tirelessly vivacious!   150
Damned wretch, in endless stupor you're prostrated!
Your lord's best happiness you've now frustrated.

Now Master That One's moodiness bemuses,
He'll not take orders nor brook any spurning,
But suddenly he's there, and quietly chooses   155
To raise himself, to splendrous form returning;
Thus freed, the traveller that parched prospect loses
Of all night by the well in thirsty burning.
He leans to kiss the sleeping girl who draws him
But stops, he feels pulled back, some power awes him.   160

Who else has spurred his strength re-animated
Than she, whose cherished value never ceases,
He wed in youth's untethered zest unsated?
Her fire anew its freshening releases,
And as, when feeble first, his torments baited   165
So now, when strong, his awed unease increases;
Then fearful, cautious, quiet, quiet, he's leaving
That zone enspelled in grace and magic's weaving.

He sits, writes: 'Near home I met with more delaying,
Chance took me further from my destination,   170
But here, in this strange place where I've been staying,
I've pledged to you my heart's re-dedication.
I'll end this letter with this secret saying:
Only by sickness is health validated.
Of many a good my words to you have spoken,   175
The best must stay in silence never broken.'

The cockerel crows. At once she swiftly pushes
The sheets off, throws her dress on, still half-dreaming.
She startles, looks, lowers her eyes and blushes,
Her being there feels strange and not quite seeming;   180
And as this final time away she rushes
His eyes still hold her lovely body's gleaming:
The post-horn sounds; he rides along in pleasure
With heart restored to greet his love and treasure.

Und weil zuletzt bei jeder Dichtungsweise   185
Moralien uns ernstlich fördern sollen,
So will auch ich in so beliebtem Gleise
Euch gern bekennen, was die Verse wollen:
Wir stolpern wohl auf unsrer Lebensreise,
Und doch vermögen in der Welt, der tollen,   190
Zwei Hebel viel aufs irdische Getriebe:
Sehr viel die *Pflicht*, unendlich mehr die *Liebe!*

[Sterbende Fliege]

Sie saugt mit Gier verrätrisches Getränke
Unabgesetzt, vom ersten Zug verführt;
Sie fühlt sich wohl, und längst sind die Gelenke
Der zarten Beinchen schon paralysiert,
Nicht mehr gewandt, die Flügelchen zu putzen,   5
Nicht mehr geschickt, das Köpfchen aufzustutzen –
Das Leben so sich im Genuß verliert.
Zum Stehen kaum wird noch das Füßchen taugen;
So schlürft sie fort, und mitten unterm Saugen
Umnebelt ihr der Tod die tausend Augen.   10

Gegenwart

Alles kündet dich an!
Erscheinet die herrliche Sonne,
Folgst du, so hoff' ich es, bald.

Trittst du im Garten hervor,
So bist du die Rose der Rosen,   5
Lilie der Lilien zugleich.

Wenn du im Tanze dich regst,
So regen sich alle Gestirne
Mit dir und um dich umher.

Nacht! und so wär' es denn Nacht!   10
Nun überscheinst du des Mondes
Lieblichen, ladenden Glanz.

And since at last all poetry's a fable   185
That needs some moral that is edifying,
My verse shall try as much as it is able
To gladly tell the point that's underlying:
In earth's mad business stumbling and unstable
We yet find much is done, there's no denying,   190
By two strong powers within us and above:
By *Duty* much, endlessly more by *Love!*

[A Dying Fly] (*1810*)

How avidly it goes on sucking steady
The treacherous drink, seduced by that first taste;
It feels so well, though paralysed already
In jointed legs minute and finely traced;
No longer agile, tiny wings to spangle,   5
No longer able little head to angle –
Thus lost in its enjoyment life must waste.
The little foot will soon be feebly listing;
And so it gulps for more, its suck persisting
As death round all its thousand eyes is misting.   10

Presence (*1812*)

All things tell when you come!
So when the sun shines in its splendour
You will, I hope, follow soon.

If in the garden you walk
Then you are the rose of all roses,   5
Lily of lilies as well

And as you move when you dance
The constellate stars will dance with you
And all around you at once.

Night! and so let it be night!   10
Now you'll outshine the moon's lovely
Luminous welcoming sheen.

Ladend und lieblich bist du,
Und Blumen, Mond und Gestirne
Huldigen, Sonne, nur dir. 15

Sonne! so sei du auch mir
Die Schöpferin herrlicher Tage;
Leben und Ewigkeit ist's.

Was wär'ein Gott, der nur von außen stieße

Was wär' ein Gott, der nur von außen stieße,
Im Kreis das All am Finger laufen ließe!
Ihm ziemt's, die Welt im Innern zu bewegen,
Natur in Sich, Sich in Natur zu hegen,
So daß, was in Ihm lebt und webt und ist, 5
Nie Seine Kraft, nie Seinen Geist vermißt.

Im Innern ist ein Universum auch;
Daher der Völker löblicher Gebrauch,
Daß jeglicher das Beste, was er kennt,
Er Gott, ja seinen Gott benennt, 10
Ihm Himmel und Erden übergibt,
Ihn fürchtet und wo möglich liebt.

Aus *Zahme Xenien* VI

Vom Vater hab ich die Statur,
Des Lebens ernstes Führen;
Vom Mütterchen die Frohnatur
Und Lust zu fabulieren.
Urahnherr war den Schönsten hold, 5
Das spukt so hin and wieder;
Urahnfrau liebte Schmuck und Gold,
Das zuckt wohl durch die Glieder.
Sind nun die Elemente nicht
Aus dem Komplex zu trennen, 10
Was ist denn an dem ganzen Wicht
Original zu nennen?

Welcoming lovely you are
And flowers, moon, and the starlight
Venerate, sun, only you.   15

Sun! be that also for me,
Creator of days of great splendour;
Life and eternity's there.

What God would nudge his world but not be in it (1812)

What God would nudge his world but not be in it
And only round his finger twirl and spin it!
He moves the world by inwardly impelling,
And He is nature's, nature His, indwelling
So that what in Him lives and works and is   5
Can't lack the power and spirit that are His.

Within us too a universe we find;
Hence, laudably, that custom of mankind
That each will give his own ideal the name
Of God, as his own God proclaim,   10
Will give Him earth and heaven above,
Will fear Him and may even love.

From *Friendly Xenia VI* (1815–27)

My stature is my Father's part,
Life's earnest from the cradle;
From Mother I've my sunny heart
And fancy for a fable.
Great-grandpa had an eye for girls,   5
At times in me it itches;
Great-grandma fancied gold and pearls,
An urge all through for riches.
These parts make up a man like me
And can't be separated,   10
So where's originality
In what a chap's created?

Frühling Übers Jahr

Das Beet schon lockert
Sich's in die Höh',
Da wanken Glöckchen
So weiß wie Schnee;
Safran entfaltet   5
Gewalt'ge Glut,
Smaragden keimt es
Und keimt wie Blut.
Primeln stolzieren
So naseweis,   10
Schalkhafte Veilchen
Versteckt mit Fleiß;
Was auch noch alles
Da regt und webt,
Genug, der Frühling   15
Er wirkt und lebt.

Doch was im Garten
Am reichsten blüht,
Das ist des Liebchens
Lieblich Gemüt.   20
Da glühen Blicke
Mir immerfort,
Erregend Liedchen,
Erheiternd Wort.
Ein immer offen,   25
Ein Blütenherz,
Im Ernste freundlich
Und rein im Scherz.
Wenn Ros' und Lilie
Der Sommer bringt,   30
Er doch vergebens
Mit Liebchen ringt.

Spring All Year Through (1816)

The loosening flower-bed
Lets itself go,
Small bells are swaying
All white as snow;
Crocus releases   5
From emerald bud
A glowing power
And burgeons blood.
Primroses pertly
Parade and prance,   10
Violet teases
And looks askance;
Whatever's stirring
With might and main,
Spring's up and doing   15
And live again.

But where the garden's
Richness excels
Is where my darling's
Dear presence dwells.   20
Those looks that warm me
And ever fire,
To song excite me,
To word inspire:
A heart that flowers,   25
That's open and clear,
In earnest kindly,
In jest sincere.
Though rose and lily
Take summer's part   30
My love's the winner
That holds my heart.

Trauerloge

An dem öden Strand des Lebens,
Wo sich Dün auf Düne häuft,
Wo der Sturm im Finstern träuft,
Setze dir ein Ziel des Strebens.
Unter schon verloschnen Siegeln   5
Tausend Väter hingestreckt,
Ach! von neuen, frischen Hügeln
Freund an Freunden überdeckt.

Hast du so dich abgefunden,
Werde Nacht und Äther klar,   10
Und der ewgen Sterne Schar
Deute dir belebte Stunden,
Wo du hier mit Ungetrübten,
Treulich wirkend, gern verweilst
Und auch treulich den geliebten   15
Ewigen entgegeneilst.

Urworte, Orphisch

ΔΑΙΜΩΝ, Dämon

Wie an dem Tag, der dich der Welt verliehen,
Die Sonne stand zum Gruße der Planeten,
Bist alsobald und fort und fort gediehen
Nach dem Gesetz, wonach du angetreten.
So mußt du sein, dir kannst du nicht entfliehen,   5
So sagten schon Sibyllen, so Propheten;
Und keine Zeit und keine Macht zerstückelt
Geprägte Form, die lebend sich entwickelt.

TYXH, Das Zufällige

Die strenge Grenze doch umgeht gefällig
Ein Wandelndes, das mit und um uns wandelt;   10
Nicht einsam bleibst du, bildest dich gesellig
Und handelst wohl so, wie ein andrer handelt:
Im Leben ist's bald hin-, bald widerfällig,
Es ist ein Tand und wird so durchgetandelt.
Schon hat sich still der Jahre Kreis geründet,   15
Die Lampe harrt der Flamme, die entzündet.

Memorial (1816)

There on shores where no life's thriving,
Where dune piles on dune in heaps,
Where the storm in darkness seeps,
Let your aim be onward striving.
Under cyphers long since smothered   5
Forebears thousandfold lie still,
Oh! now new fresh mounds have covered
Friend on friends in death's deep chill.

Thus accept our life so fated
Then may night and sky grow bright   10
And stars' thronged eternal light
Mean to you hours animated,
Whilst with others here untroubled
You stay loyal, active, kind
Hurrying with love redoubled   15
Loved eternal ones to find.

Primal Words, Orphic (1817)

ΔΑΙΜΩΝ, Daimon

When you were granted here your brief admission,
As sun and planets met that day they charted
For evermore your growing to fruition
According to the law by which you started.
Thus must you be, from self there's no remission,   5
Thus long have sibyls, prophets this imparted;
Nor any time nor any power can shatter
Imprinted form informing living matter.

TYXH, Chance

But easing change gets round that stern constriction
As with and round us change is all-imbuing;   10
No more alone, you grow through social friction
And do such deeds as any man is doing.
This life's an ebb and flow, a contradiction,
A toy that's toyed with, play for our pursuing.
The years have quitely formed the circle's essence,   15
The lamp awaits the flame of incandescence.

ΕΡΩΣ, *Liebe*

Die bleibt nicht aus! – Er stürzt vom Himmel nieder,
Wohin er sich aus alter Öde schwang,
Er schwebt heran auf luftigem Gefieder
Um Stirn und Brust den Frühlingstag entlang,   20
Scheint jetzt zu fliehn, vom Fliehen kehrt er wieder,
Da wird ein Wohl im Weh, so süß und bang.
Gar manches Herz verschwebt im Allgemeinen,
Doch widmet sich das edelste dem Einen.

ΑΝΑΓΚΗ, *Nötigung*

Da ist's denn wieder, wie die Sterne wollten: 25
Bedingung und Gesetz; und aller Wille
Ist nur ein Wollen, weil wir eben sollten,
Und vor dem Willen schweigt die Willkür stille;
Das Liebste wird vom Herzen weggescholten,
Dem harten Muß bequemt sich Will' und Grille.   30
So sind wir scheinfrei denn nach manchen Jahren
Nur enger dran, als wir am Anfang waren.

ΕΛΠΙΣ, *Hoffnung*

Doch solcher Grenze, solcher eh'rnen Mauer
Höchst widerwärt'ge Pforte wird entriegelt,
Sie stehe nur mit alter Felsendauer!   35
Ein Wesen regt sich leicht und ungezügelt:
Aus Wolkendecke, Nebel, Regenschauer
Erhebt sie uns, mit ihr, durch sie beflügelt;
Ihr kennt sie wohl, sie schwärmt durch alle Zonen;
Ein Flügelschlag – und hinter uns Äonen.   40

Um Mitternacht

Um Mitternacht ging ich, nicht eben gerne,
Klein, kleiner Knabe, jenen Kirchhof hin
Zu Vaters Haus, des Pfarrers; Stern am Sterne
Sie leuchteten doch alle gar zu schön;
    Um Mitternacht.   5

Wenn ich dann ferner in des Lebens Weite
Zur Liebsten mußte, mußte, weil sie zog,
Gestirn und Nordschein über mir im Streite,

ΕΡΩΣ, *Love*

And come it must! – He plunges earthwards winging
Who from the timeless void to heaven once sped,
On airy pinions hovering and swinging
All springtime's day around the heart and head,   20
Away and back again forever springing,
Then woe is weal, there's sweet delights in dread.
So many soaring hearts are dissipated,
The noblest to the One is dedicated.

ΑΝΑΓΚΗ, *Necessity*

Then back once more, to what the stars had fated: 25
Conditioning and law; and wish from willing
Can only come since we are obligated,
Our will then all our fitful fancies killing;
Its dearest from the heart is extirpated,
Hard 'Must' prevails, both will and fancy stilling.   30
Thus, though we seem free, yet constrictions bind us
More closely still than those that first confined us.

ΕΛΠΙΣ, *Hope*

But such a confine, such a wall immuring
In odious chafe, is breached and left ungated
Though like the timeless crags it seem enduring!   35
A Being rises light and liberated:
Through showering rain and cloud and mist obscuring
She lifts us up, we soar on wings elated:
You know her well, ranging all zones to find us;
One wingbeat – and the aeons lie behind us!   40

At Midnight (*1818*)

At midnight I would walk, but very wary,
Across that churchyard, such a small small boy,
To father's house, the parson's; stars all starry,
Their really lovely sparkling was such joy;
　　At midnight.   5

And when I later then in life's extension
Was forced to her, was forced by love's intent,
The stars and Northern Lights in high contention,

Ich gehend, kommend Seligkeiten sog;
    Um Mitternacht.   10

Bis dann zuletzt des vollen Mondes Helle
So klar und deutlich mir ins Finstere drang,
Auch der Gedanke willig, sinnig, schnelle
Sich ums Vergangne wie ums Künftige schlang;
    Um Mitternacht.   15

Epirrhema

Müsset im Naturbetrachten
Immer eins wie alles achten;
Nichts ist drinnen, nichts ist draußen:
Denn was innen, das ist außen.
So ergreifet ohne Säumnis   5
Heilig öffentlich Geheimnis.

*

Freuet euch des wahren Scheins,
Euch des ernsten Spieles:
Kein Lebendiges ist ein Eins,
Immer ist's ein Vieles.   10

Antepirrhema

So schauet mit bescheidnem Blick
Der ewigen Weberin Meisterstück,
Wie Ein Tritt tausend Fäden regt,
Die Schifflein hinüber, herüber schießen,
Die Fäden sich begegnend fließen,   5
Ein Schlag tausend Verbindungen schlägt,
Das hat sie nicht zusammengebettelt,
Sie hat's von Ewigkeit angezettelt;
Damit der ewige Meistermann
Getrost den Einschlag werfen kann.   10

I'd savour coming blisses as I went;
    At midnight.   10

Until at last the moon in fullness shining
My darkness pierced, so clearly and defined;
Then thought, all willing, sensing, leaped combining
Both past and and future instantly in mind;
    At midnight.   15

Epirrhema[12] (*1819*)

If you'd look at nature truly
One as all examine duly!
No thing's inside, outside neither:
In is out and both are either.
Grasp it quick, let nought confound you,   5
Sacred secret all around you.

      *

True appearance, earnest game,
Joys in them discover:
Nothing living is one and the same,
It's always many another!   10

Antepirrhema (*1819*)

Now humbly observe as she without cease
Eternally weaves her masterpiece,
One tread, a thousand threads respond,
The shuttles shoot swiftly to and froing,
The joining threads run onwards flowing,   5
One throw a thousand links will bond!
She hasn't just now scraped that together,
In eternity she planned it for ever;
So that the eternal craftsman will know
That all is well when he makes his throw.   10

St Nepomuks Vorabend

Karlsbad, den 15 Mai 1820

Lichtlein schwimmen auf dem Strome,
Kinder singen auf der Brücken,
Glocke, Glöckchen fügt vom Dome
Sich der Andacht, dem Entzücken.

Lichtlein schwinden, Sterne schwinden;   5
Also löste sich die Seele
Unsres Heil'gen, nicht verkünden
Durft' er anvertraute Fehle.

Lichtlein, schwimmet! Spielt, ihr Kinder!
Kinder-Chor, o singe, singe!   10
Und verkündiget nicht minder,
Was den Stern zu Sternen bringe.

Wilhelm Tischbeins Idyllen

I

Würdige Prachtgebäude stürzen,
Mauer fällt, Gewölbe bleiben,
Daß nach tausendjähr'gem Treiben
Tor und Pfeiler sich verkürzen.
Dann beginnt das Leben wieder,   5
Boden mischt sich neuen Saaten,
Rank' auf Ranke senkt sich nieder;
Der Natur ist's wohl geraten.

II

Schön und menschlich ist der Geist,
Der uns in das Freie weist,
Wo in Wäldern, auf der Flur,
Wie im steilen Berggehänge,
Sonnenauf – und – untergänge   5
Preisen Gott und die Natur.

III

Wenn in Wäldern Baum an Bäumen,
Bruder sich mit Bruder nähret,
Sei das Wandern, sei das Träumen
Unverwehrt und ungestöret:

Eve of St Nepomuk[13] (1820)

Karlsbad, 15 May 1820

Lanterns float downstream a-twinkle,
Children on the bridge are singing,
Big bell, small bell, peal and tinkle,
All delight and reverence ringing.

Lanterns fade, the stars are fading;   5
So was loosed the soul sure-guided
Of our saint, whom no persuading
Forced to speak of faults confided.

Lanterns, float on! children, play then!
Children's choir, o sing it singing!   10
And no less proclaim and say then
Why this star to stars is winging.

Wilhelm Tischbein's Idylls (1821)

I

Noble splendid buildings tumble,
Walls collapse round vaults still standing,
After centuries commanding
Entrances and pillars crumble.
Life then starts itself restoring,   5
Earth and new seed mix together,
Roots send roots deep downwards boring;
Nature delves and builds as ever.

II

See this mind humane, serene,
Showing us the open scene
Where in woods, on meadow graze,
In steep mountain chasms yawning,
Sunset and the sunrise dawning   5
Offer God and nature praise.

III

Woods with trees and trees are teeming
Nourished, brotherly, contented,
Apt for wandering, apt for dreaming
Undisturbed and unprevented;

Doch, wo einzelne Gesellen
Zierlich miteinander streben,
Sich zum schönen Ganzen stellen,
Das ist Freude, das ist Leben.   5

IV

Mitten in dem Wasserspiegel
Hob die Eiche sich empor,
Majestätisch Fürstensiegel
Solchem grünen Waldesflor;
Sieht sich selbst zu ihren Füßen,   5
Schaut den Himmel in der Flut:
So des Lebens zu genießen
Einsamkeit ist höchstes Gut.

V

Edel-ernst, ein Halbtier, liegend,
Im Beschauen, im Besinnen,
Hin und her im Geiste wiegend,
Denkt er Großes zu gewinnen.
Ach, er möchte gern entfliehen   5
Solchem Auftrag, solcher Würde;
Einen Helden zu erziehen
Wird Centauren selbst zur Bürde.

VI

Was wir froh und dankbar fühlen,
Wenn es auch am Ende quält,
Was wir lechzen zu erzielen,
Wo es Herz und Sinnen fehlt:
Heitre Gegend, groß gebildet,   5
Jugendschritt an Freundesbrust,
Wechselseitig abgemildet,
Holder Liebe Schmerzenslust;
Alles habt ihr nun empfangen,
Irdisch war's und in der Näh';   10
Sehnsucht aber und Verlangen
Hebt vom Boden in die Höh'.
An der Quelle sind's Najaden,
Sind Sylphiden in der Luft,
Leichter fühlt ihr euch im Baden,   15
Leichter noch in Himmelsduft;
Und das Plätschern und das Wallen

Where companions, though they're single   5
Gracefully compete in presence
And to beauty's wholeness mingle,
That is joy, and that's life's essence.

IV

In the water's mirror tinted
Oak has raised itself on high,
Princely seal majestic printed
On such greening woods close by,
Sees below them its reflection,   5
In the water sees the skies:
Life enjoying to perfection,
Solitude's most precious prize.

V

Noble, grave, a half-beast lying
In recall, in contemplation,
Ponders courses multiplying,
Serving greatness his vocation.
Ah, he'd like to lose the galling   5
Burden of a hero's mentor;
Such an honour, such a calling,
Weighs down even for a centaur.

VI

Feeling grateful joy outbursting
Though it end on torment's rack,
Reaching all for which we're thirsting,
All our hearts and senses lack:
Large conception, landscape pleasing,   5
Youth steps out, in fond embrace,
Mutual each other easing,
Painful joy of love's fair grace;
All has now to you been given,
Earthly gifts, all close nearby;   10
But then yearning wants are driven
Leaving earth to rise on high.
Those are sylphs where sky is brighter,
Naiads where the fresh spring plays,
In the bathing you feel lighter,   15
Lighter still in heavenly haze;
Gliding, splashing and cascading,

Ein und andres zieht euch an;
Lasset Lied und Bild verhallen,
Doch im Innern ist's getan.   20

VII

Ruhig Wasser, grause Höhle,
Bergeshöh' und ernstes Licht,
Seltsam, wie es unsrer Seele
Schauderhafte Laute spricht.
So erweist sich wohl Natur,   5
Künstlerblick vernimmt es nur.

Eins und Alles

Im Grenzenlosen sich zu finden,
Wird gern der Einzelne verschwinden,
Da löst sich aller Überdruß;
Statt heißem Wünschen, wildem Wollen,
Statt läst'gem Fordern, strengem Sollen,   5
Sich aufzugeben ist Genuß.

Weltseele, komm, uns zu durchdringen!
Dann mit dem Weltgeist selbst zu ringen
Wird unsrer Kräfte Hochberuf.
Teilnehmend führen gute Geister,   10
Gelinde leitend, höchste Meister,
Zu dem, der alles schafft und schuf.

Und umzuschaffen das Geschaffne,
Damit sich's nicht zum Starren waffne,
Wirkt ewiges lebendiges Tun.   15
Und was nicht war, nun will es werden,
Zu reinen Sonnen, farbigen Erden,
In keinem Falle darf es ruhn.

Es soll sich regen, schaffend handeln,
Erst sich gestalten, dann verwandeln;   20
Nur scheinbar steht's Momente still.
Das Ewige regt sich fort in allen,
Denn alles muß in Nichts zerfallen,
Wenn es im Sein beharren will.

Each attracts and draws you on;
Words and images are fading
But within the work's been done.   20

VII

Water calm, dark caves' recesses,
Solemn light and mountain peaks,
Strange how this our soul addresses
And with awesome import speaks.
Nature thus herself has shown,   5
Sensed by artist's eye alone.

One and All[14] (October 1821)

To find ourselves in boundless being
Who would not vanish, gladly fleeing
From all that wearies and annoys;
No ardent wants, no wild desiring,
No duties strict, no orders tiring,   5
Such self-surrender each enjoys.

World-soul, come, let your force pervade us!
To combat the world-spirit aid us
And match our powers to these high stakes.
Then sympathetic spirits guide us,   10
As gentle masters walk beside us
To him who all things made and makes.

To take what's made and then re-make it,
To fight rigidity and break it,
Eternal living action quests.   15
What never was grows real and fuller
As pure clear suns, as worlds with colour,
And in becoming never rests.

It all must move, make new creations,
First take on form, then transformations;   20
For moments it just seems held fast.
In all things life's perpetuated,
And all must be annihilated
That in existence strives to last.

Trilogie der Leidenschaft

An Werther

Noch einmal wagst du, vielbeweinter Schatten,
Hervor dich an das Tageslicht,
Begegnest mir auf neu beblümten Matten,
Und meinen Anblick scheust du nicht.
Es ist, als ob du lebtest in der Frühe,   5
Wo uns der Tau auf Einem Feld erquickt,
Und nach des Tages unwillkommner Mühe
Der Scheidesonne letzter Strahl entzückt;
Zum Bleiben ich, zum Scheiden du erkoren,
Gingst du voran – und hast nicht viel verloren.   10

Des Menschen Leben scheint ein herrlich Los:
Der Tag wie lieblich, so die Nacht wie groß!
Und wir, gepflanzt in Paradieses Wonne,
Genießen kaum der hocherlauchten Sonne,
Da kämpft sogleich verworrene Bestrebung   15
Bald mit uns selbst und bald mit der Umgebung;
Keins wird vom andern wünschenswert ergänzt,
Von außen düstert's, wenn es innen glänzt,
Ein glänzend Äußres deckt mein trüber Blick,
Da steht es nah – und man verkennt das Glück.   20

Nun glauben wir's zu kennen! Mit Gewalt
Ergreift uns Liebreiz weiblicher Gestalt:
Der Jüngling, froh wie in der Kindheit Flor,
Im Frühling tritt als Frühling selbst hervor,
Entzückt, erstaunt, wer dies ihm angetan?   25
Er schaut umher, die Welt gehört ihm an.
Ins Weite zieht ihn unbefangne Hast,
Nichts engt ihn ein, nicht Mauer, nicht Palast;
Wie Vögelschar an Wäldergipfeln streift,
So schwebt auch er, der um die Liebste schweift,   30
Er sucht vom Äther, den er gern verläßt,
Den treuen Blick, und dieser hält ihn fest.

Doch erst zu früh und dann zu spät gewarnt,
Fühlt er den Flug gehemmt, fühlt sich umgarnt,
Das Wiedersehn ist froh, das Scheiden schwer,   35
Das Wieder-Wiedersehn beglückt noch mehr,
Und Jahre sind im Augenblick ersetzt;
Doch tückisch harrt das Lebewohl zuletzt.

Trilogy of Passion (1823–4)

To Werther

Lamented shade, once more with unsure greeting
You venture to the light of day,
Here on new-flowered meadows we are meeting;
This time you do not shrink away.
It is as if you lived when all was starting,   5
When dew upon One field our life can mend
And when the sun enraptures us in parting
With one last ray as day's drear labours end;
I stayed, you left, our fate and not our choosing,
You went before – how little you were losing.   10

The life of man seems such a splendid fate;
The day how fair, and night as well how great!
And we, in this sheer Paradise so favoured,
The sun's magnificence we've hardly savoured
When our own striving muddles and confounds us   15
Now with ourselves and now with all around us;
And neither complements the other quite,
It's dark without when all within gleams bright,
And outward bright goes dulled before my eyes,
So near – the happiness we do not prize.   20

And now we think we see! By force compelled
In love of women's image we are held:
The youth, as happy as when childhood blooms,
In spring the form of spring itself assumes,
Enrapt, amazed, who worked such spell as this?   25
He looks around, and all the world is his.
Unfettered haste impels his onward need,
No wall, no palace, nothing can impede;
As flocking birds round woodland summits fly
He hovers round his love and keeps close by,   30
And glad to leave the air, he seeks and finds
The faithful look, and this it is that binds.

But warned at first too soon and then too late
He feels his flight is checked, ensnared by fate,
To meet again is joy, to part is sore,   35
Again to meet again is joy still more,
One moment can replace long years that passed;
But farewell's patient malice wins at last.

Du lächelst, Freund, gefühlvoll, wie sich ziemt:
Ein gräßlich Scheiden machte dich berühmt; 40
Wir feierten dein kläglich Mißgeschick,
Du ließest uns zu Wohl und Weh zurück;
Dann zog uns wieder ungewisse Bahn
Der Leidenschaften labyrinthisch an;
Und wir, verschlungen wiederholter Not, 45
Dem Scheiden endlich – Scheiden ist der Tod!
Wie klingt es rührend, wenn der Dichter singt,
Den Tod zu meiden, den das Scheiden bringt!
Verstrickt in solche Qualen, halbverschuldet,
Geb' ihm ein Gott zu sagen, was er duldet. 50

Elegie

Und wenn der Mensch in seiner Qual verstummt
Gab mir ein Gott zu sagen, was ich leide.

Was soll ich nun vom Wiedersehen hoffen,
Von dieses Tages noch geschloßner Blüte?
Das Paradies, die Hölle steht dir offen;
Wie wankelsinnig regt sich's im Gemüte! –
Kein Zweifeln mehr! Sie tritt ans Himmelstor, 5
Zu ihren Armen hebt sie dich empor.

So warst du denn im Paradies empfangen,
Als wärst du wert des ewig schönen Lebens;
Dir blieb kein Wunsch, kein Hoffen, kein Verlangen,
Hier war das Ziel des innigsten Bestrebens, 10
Und in dem Anschaun dieses einzig Schönen
Versiegte gleich der Quell sehnsüchtiger Tränen.

Wie regte nicht der Tag die raschen Flügel,
Schien die Minuten vor sich her zu treiben!
Der Abendkuß, ein treu verbindlich Siegel: 15
So wird es auch der nächsten Sonne bleiben.
Die Stunden glichen sich in zartem Wandern
Wie Schwestern zwar, doch keine ganz den andern.

Der Kuß, der letzte, grausam süß, zerschneidend
Ein herrliches Geflecht verschlungner Minnen. 20
Nun eilt, nun stockt der Fuß, die Schwelle meidend,
Als trieb' ein Cherub flammend ihn von hinnen;
Das Auge starrt auf düstrem Pfad verdrossen,
Es blickt zurück, die Pforte steht verschlossen.

You smile, my friend, with feeling, as is due:
A fearsome parting brought such fame for you;   40
Memorials to your piteous fate we show,
You left us here behind for weal or woe;
Then we once more were drawn into the maze
Of chartless passion's labyrinthine ways;
And we, enmeshed in pains that multiply,   45
At last to parting – parting is to die!
How moving always when the poet sings
To side-step death which every parting brings!
In torments snared of his half-guilt's procuring
May some god help him say what he's enduring.   50

Elegy

And while mankind is silent in its pain
A god gave me to say all that I suffer.

Now from our meeting what can be expected,
From this new day whose flowering's not yet ready?
In Paradise received, to Hell rejected;
How changeable my thoughts, my heart unsteady! –
She stands at Heaven's gate! Away with qualms!   5
She lifts you up and takes you to her arms.

So Paradise, as if you'd earned your standing,
And life forever beautiful you entered;
No need to wish, to hope, no more demanding,
The end on which your inward struggling centred;   10
As you this signal beauty contemplated
The source of all your yearning tears abated.

On what quick wings the day pursued its chases
And drove the minutes on its course swift-flighted!
The evening kiss, a seal on your embraces;   15
Until the next sun so you stay united.
Like gentle sisters hour with hour assembled
And each, though not completely, each resembled.

The kiss, the last one, sweet and anguished, shearing
A weave of love so marvellously connected.   20
Foot runs, holds back, never the threshold nearing,
As though by Cherubim in flames ejected;
Eye stares on sombre path as torments blind it,
Looks back once more, the gate stays closed behind it.

Und nun verschlossen in sich selbst, als hätte   25
Dies Herz sich nie geöffnet, selige Stunden
Mit jedem Stern des Himmels um die Wette
An ihrer Seite leuchtend nicht empfunden;
Und Mißmut, Reue, Vorwurf, Sorgenschwere
Belasten's nun in schwüler Atmosphäre.   30

Ist denn die Welt nicht übrig? Felsenwände,
Sind sie nicht mehr gekrönt von heiligen Schatten?
Die Ernte, reift sie nicht? Ein grün Gelände,
Zieht sich's nicht hin am Fluß durch Busch und Matten?
Und wölbt sich nicht das überweltlich Große,   35
Gestaltenreiche, bald Gestaltenlose?

Wie leicht und zierlich, klar und zart gewoben
Schwebt, seraphgleich, aus ernster Wolken Chor,
Als glich' es ihr, am blauen Äther droben,
Ein schlank Gebild aus lichtem Duft empor;   40
So sahst du sie in frohem Tanze walten,
Die lieblichste der lieblichsten Gestalten.

Doch nur Momente darfst dich unterwinden,
Ein Luftgebild statt ihrer festzuhalten;
Ins Herz zurück, dort wirst du's besser finden,   45
Dort regt sie sich in wechselnden Gestalten;
Zu vielen bildet Eine sich hinüber,
So tausendfach und immer, immer lieber.

Wie zum Empfang sie an den Pforten weilte
Und mich von dannauf stufenweis beglückte;   50
Selbst nach dem letzten Kuß mich noch ereilte,
Den letztesten mir auf die Lippen drückte:
So klar beweglich bleibt das Bild der Lieben,
Mit Flammenschrift ins treue Herz geschrieben.

Ins Herz, das fest wie zinnenhohe Mauer   55
Sich ihr bewahrt und sie in sich bewahret,
Für sie sich freut an seiner eignen Dauer,
Nur weiß von sich, wenn sie sich offenbaret,
Sich freier fühlt in so geliebten Schranken
Und nur noch schlägt, für alles ihr zu danken.   60

War Fähigkeit zu lieben, war Bedürfen
Von Gegenliebe weggelöscht, verschwunden;

This heart is also closed, as if denying   25
That it had ever opened, no more minding
Those hours with all the constellations vying
When by her side it felt her radiance binding;
By cares, bad mood, remorse, reproach it's covered,
In sultry atmosphere oppressed and smothered.   30

But is the world not left? Those high crags shaded,
Is there not still on them a sacred presence?
The harvest not still ripening? Still unfaded
Through woods and fields the riverside's green pleasance?
And is there not on high that vastness rounding,   35
Now formlessness and now all forms abounding?

How light and delicate, how clear and tender,
From solemn clouds, seraphic, soaring high,
In lucid haze there floats an image slender,
As if herself, in blue ethereal sky;   40
So once you used to see her supreme dancing,
Of most entrancing forms the most entrancing.

But only moments dare you risk the danger
To grasp not her but mere hallucinations;
Within your heart, that's where you'll feel no stranger,   45
That's where she moves in forms and transformations;
To many One evolves through changing stages,
Thus thousandfold, and more and more engages.

The way she looked when by the gates she waited
And then on rising steps enhanced my rapture;   50
As when with one last kiss we separated
And back she ran the lastest kiss to capture:
Love's image clear and changing keeps returning,
Into this faithful heart its imprint burning,

This heart which keeps with castle-walled assurance   55
Itself for her, and her within is holding,
For her is gladdened by its own endurance,
Self-knowing only in her self-unfolding,
That feels such dear constraints are truly freeing
And only beats to thank her for all being.   60

The power to love was gone, all gone the needing
Of love's response outflowing from another;

Ist Hoffnungslust zu freudigen Entwürfen,
Entschlüssen, rascher Tat sogleich gefunden!
Wenn Liebe je den Liebenden begeistet,   65
Ward es an mir aufs lieblichste geleistet;

Und zwar durch sie! – Wie lag ein innres Bangen
Auf Geist und Körper, unwillkommner Schwere:
Von Schauerbildern rings der Blick umfangen
Im wüsten Raum beklommner Herzensleere;   70
Nun dämmert Hoffnung von bekannter Schwelle,
Sie selbst erscheint in milder Sonnenhelle.

Dem Frieden Gottes, welcher euch hienieden
Mehr als Vernunft beseliget – wir lesen's – ,
Vergleich' ich wohl der Liebe heitern Frieden   75
In Gegenwart des allgeliebten Wesens;
Da ruht das Herz, und nichts vermag zu stören
Den tiefsten Sinn, den Sinn, ihr zu gehören.

In unsers Busens Reine wogt ein Streben,
Sich einem Höhern, Reinen, Unbekannten   80
Aus Dankbarkeit freiwillig hinzugeben,
Enträtselnd sich den ewig Ungenannten;
Wir heißen's: fromm sein! – Solcher seligen Höhe
Fühl' ich mich teilhaft, wenn ich vor ihr stehe.

Vor ihrem Blick, wie vor der Sonne Walten,   85
Vor ihrem Atem, wie vor Frühlingslüften,
Zerschmilzt, so längst sich eisig starr gehalten,
Der Selbstsinn tief in winterlichen Grüften;
Kein Eigennutz, kein Eigenwille dauert,
Vor ihrem Kommen sind sie weggeschauert.   90

Es ist, als wenn sie sagte: 'Stund' um Stunde
Wird uns das Leben freundlich dargeboten,
Das Gestrige ließ uns geringe Kunde,
Das Morgende, zu wissen ist's verboten;
Und wenn ich je mich vor dem Abend scheute,   95
Die Sonne sank und sah noch, was mich freute.

Drum tu wie ich und schaue, froh-verständig,
Dem Augenblick ins Auge! Kein Verschieben!
Begegn' ihm schnell, wohlwollend wie lebendig,
Im Handeln sei's, zur Freude, sei's dem Lieben;   100

Then hopes, bright plans, resolve, the deed succeeding,
Again the zest of living I discover!
If ever love was lover's inspiration   65
It gave in me a lovely demonstration;

And all through her! – A fearful indecision
Oppressed the mind and body, all frustrated:
Grim spectres all around the prisoned vision
In anxious heartvoid's wasteland desolated;   70
The threshold now with gleams of hope is clearing
As she in gentle sunshine is appearing.

The peace of God, more happiness bestowing
Than all our understanding – scripture tells us –
Can be compared with peace that comes from knowing   75
The loved one's presence that serenely quells us;
The heart's at rest, nought mars the deep, deep feeling
That we belong to her for life and healing.

Towards a Higher, Purer, Unknown driven
We sense our purity of heart inclining   80
In grateful self-surrender freely given,
The Evernameless-One thereby divining;
We call this: reverence! – Just so I adore her
And it is ecstasy to stand before her.

Her look, as with the sun's commanding vigour,   85
Her breath as when I sense the springtime breezes
Dissolves the icy egotistic rigour
Of self that in its wintered caverns freezes;
No self-will, no self-serving, all that's vanished,
All by her coming swept away and banished.   90

It is as if she said: 'See hour by hour
How kindly to our share in life we're bidden,
What stays from yesterday has little power,
To know what comes tomorrow is forbidden;
And if the thought of evening uneased me   95
The sun went down and I saw much that pleased me.

So do like me and look, with sense and brightly,
The moment in the eye! And no protracting!
Engage it quick, approvingly and sprightly,
For pleasure, be it loving, be it acting;   100

Nur wo du bist, sei alles, immer kindlich,
So bist du alles, bist unüberwindlich.'

Du hast gut reden, dacht' ich, zum Geleite
Gab dir ein Gott die Gunst des Augenblickes,
Und jeder fühlt an deiner holden Seite   105
Sich augenblicks den Günstling des Geschickes;
Mich schreckt der Wink, von dir mich zu entfernen,
Was hilft es mir, so hohe Weisheit lernen!

Nun bin ich fern! Der jetzigen Minute,
Was ziemt denn der? Ich wüßt' es nicht zu sagen;   110
Sie bietet mir zum Schönen manches Gute,
Das lastet nur, ich muß mich ihm entschlagen;
Mich treibt umher ein unbezwinglich Sehnen,
Da bleibt kein Rat als grenzenlose Tränen.

So quellt denn fort und fließet unaufhaltsam!   115
Doch nie geläng's, die innre Glut zu dämpfen!
Schon rast's und reißt in meiner Brust gewaltsam,
Wo Tod und Leben grausend sich bekämpfen.
Wohl Kräuter gäb's, des Körpers Qual zu stillen;
Allein dem Geist fehlt's am Entschluß und Willen,   120

Fehlt's am Begriff: wie sollt' er sie vermissen?
Er wiederholt ihr Bild zu tausendmalen.
Das zaudert bald, bald wird es weggerissen,
Undeutlich jetzt und jetzt im reinsten Strahlen;
Wie könnte dies geringstem Troste frommen,   125
Die Ebb' und Flut, das Gehen wie das Kommen?

Verlaßt mich hier, getreue Weggenossen!
Laßt mich allein am Fels, in Moor und Moos;
Nur immer zu! euch ist die Welt erschlossen,
Die Erde weit, der Himmel hehr und groß;   130
Betrachtet, forscht, die Einzelheiten sammelt,
Naturgeheimnis werde nachgestammelt.

Mir ist das All, ich bin mir selbst verloren,
Der ich noch erst den Göttern Liebling war;
Sie prüften mich, verliehen mir Pandoren,   135
So reich an Gütern, reicher an Gefahr;
Sie drängten mich zum gabeseligen Munde,
Sie trennen mich, und richten mich zu Grunde.

Be so, be always childlike, wheresoever,
So you'll be everything, defeated never.'

Well you may talk, I thought, a god did guide you,
To know the moment's favour you were gifted,
The moment any man can walk beside you   105
He feels like fortune's favourite uplifted;
I shudder at the hint of separation,
How am I helped by wisdom's education!

And now I'm far away! Take now this minute;
What's right for it? I don't know how to use it;   110
It has so much of good and beauty in it
And yet it burdens, so I must refuse it;
A longing goads me that's past all containing,
These endless tears my only help remaining.

So pour unstaunchable and flow unending!   115
But for the inward fire there's nought assuages!
Already in the storm my heart is rending
Where such grim war of death and life enrages.
With herbs the body's torments may be treated;
Without resolve and will the mind's defeated,   120

Without the thought; how give up her existence?
A thousand times her image it's defining.
It hesitates, is dragged off to the distance,
Now indistinct and now the purest shining;
But what's the use, what profit is it showing,   125
This ebb and flow, the coming and the going?

So leave me here, dear friends on all my travels!
Leave me alone in rocks and moor and heath;
Press on! For you the world itself unravels,
The sky sublime and great, wide earth beneath;   130
Examine, look, sift all the detail cluttered,
Let nature's secret haltingly be uttered.

The world's all lost, myself as well I'm losing,
I, once the favourite of the gods on high;
They tested me, for me Pandora choosing,   135
So rich in gifts, in her more dangers lie;
They urged me to that generous mouth to fate me,
They separate me and annihilate me.

Aussöhnung

Die Leidenschaft bringt Leiden! – Wer beschwichtigt
Beklommnes Herz, das allzuviel verloren?
Wo sind die Stunden, überschnell verflüchtigt?
Vergebens war das Schönste dir erkoren!
Trüb' ist der Geist, verworren das Beginnen;   5
Die hehre Welt, wie schwindet sie den Sinnen!

Da schwebt hervor Musik mit Engelschwingen,
Verflicht zu Millionen Tön' um Töne,
Des Menschen Wesen durch und durch zu dringen,
Zu überfüllen ihn mit ew'ger Schöne: 10
Das Auge netzt sich, fühlt im höhern Sehnen
Den Götterwert der Töne wie der Tränen.

Und so das Herz erleichtert merkt behende,
Daß es noch lebt und schlägt und möchte schlagen,
Zum reinsten Dank der überreichen Spende   15
Sich selbst erwidernd willig darzutragen.
Da fühlte sich – o daß es ewig bliebe! –
Das Doppelglück der Töne wie der Liebe.

Der Bräutigam

Um Mitternacht, ich schlief, im Busen wachte
Das liebevolle Herz, als wär' es Tag;
Der Tag erschien, mir war, als ob es nachte,
Was ist es mir, so viel er bringen mag.

Sie fehlte ja, mein emsig Tun und Streben   5
Für sie allein ertrug ich's durch die Glut
Der heißen Stunde, welch erquicktes Leben
Am kühlen Abend! lohnend war's und gut.

Die Sonne sank, und Hand in Hand verpflichtet
Begrüßten wir den letzten Segensblick,   10
Und Auge sprach, ins Auge klar gerichtet:
Von Osten, hoffe nur, sie kommt zurück.

Um Mitternacht! der Sterne Glanz geleitet
In holdem Traum zur Schwelle, wo sie ruht.
O sei auch mir dort auszuruhn bereitet,   15
Wie es auch sei das Leben es ist gut.

Reconciliation

All passion has its pain! – Who stills the anguish
When by too great a loss the heart is riven?
Where gone the hours, so overquick to languish?
In vain to you was beauty's acme given!
The spirit drear, the muddled will's pretences;   5
The world sublime all slipping from the senses!

Then vibrant music soars on wings supernal,
A million weave of tones round tones creating
And so with beauty's overcharge eternal
All through and through man's being penetrating: 10
The eye is moistened, through a higher yearning
The power divine of tones and tears discerning.

Relieved, the supple heart then senses surely
Its beat, its eager beat, its life resurgent;
In gratitude itself it offers purely,   15
To bounteous gift makes its response convergent.
And then was sensed – oh could it last for ever! –
The double bliss of tones and love together.

The Bridegroom (1824)

At midnight's edge, I slept, by love alerted
My heart kept watch, as if it were the day;
Day came and seemed, I felt, a night deserted,
What can it be to me, bring what it may.

She was not there, my eager doings and striving   5
Were all for her as I withstood
The scorching hours, then what a fresh reviving
In evening's coolness! full reward and good.

The sun went down, and hand in hand united
We watched its final benediction burn,   10
And eye spoke clear to eye in silence plighted:
From Eastward, only hope, it will return.

At midnight's edge! in starlit radiance driven
Blessed dream abords the threshold where she rests.
O there at last to rest let me be given.   15
How good life is, however much it tests.

[Schillers Reliquien]

Im ernsten Beinhaus war's, wo ich beschaute,
  Wie Schädel Schädeln angeordnet paßten;
  Die alte Zeit gedacht ich, die ergraute.
Sie stehn in Reih' geklemmt, die sonst sich haßten,
  Und derbe Knochen, die sich tödlich schlugen,   5
  Sie liegen kreuzweis zahm allhier zu rasten.
Entrenkte Schulterblätter! was sie trugen,
  Fragt niemand mehr, und zierlich-tät'ge Glieder,
  Die Hand, der Fuß, zerstreut aus Lebensfugen.
Ihr Müden also lagt vergebens nieder,   10
  Nicht Ruh' im Grabe ließ man euch, vertrieben
  Seid ihr herauf zum lichten Tage wieder,
Und niemand kann die dürre Schale lieben,
  Welch herrlich edlen Kern sie auch bewahrte.
  Doch mir Adepten war die Schrift geschrieben,   15
Die heil'gen Sinn nicht jedem offenbarte,
  Als ich inmitten solcher starren Menge
  Unschätzbar herrlich ein Gebild gewahrte,
Daß in des Raumes Moderkält' und Enge
  Ich frei und wärmefühlend mich erquickte,   20
  Als ob ein Lebensquell dem Tod entspränge.
Wie mich geheimnisvoll die Form entzückte!
  Die gottgedachte Spur, die sich erhalten!
  Ein Blick, der mich an jenes Meer entrückte,
Das flutend strömt gesteigerte Gestalten.   25
  Geheim Gefäß! Orakelsprüche spendend,
  Wie bin ich wert, dich in der Hand zu halten,
Dich höchsten Schatz aus Moder fromm entwendend
  Und in die freie Luft zu freiem Sinnen,
  Zum Sonnenlicht andächtig hin mich wendend.   30
Was kann der Mensch im Leben mehr gewinnen,
  Als daß sich Gott-Natur ihm offenbare?
  Wie sie das Feste läßt zu Geist verrinnen,
  Wie sie das Geisterzeugte fest bewahre.

[Schiller's Remains – 1826]

In solemn charnel house I stood, surveying
  The order skulls on matching skulls attested;
  I called to mind the old times, gone and greying.
They stand tight-ranked, of former hates divested,
  And hulkish bones to mutual death once battered   5
  Lie tame in this skewed mingle to be rested.
Splayed shoulder-blades! who asks, now they are scattered,
  What once they carried! lissom limbs that sported,
  The hand, the foot, their living join is shattered.
You tired bones, still seeking rest yet thwarted,   10
  Denied the grave's deep peace, and once more driven
  To day's clear light in jumbled wrack distorted;
And no man loves the husk, dried out and riven,
  Despite the noble core it once was bearing.
  But here to me, adept, the script was given   15
Whose sacred sense was not for common sharing
  When in that press of rigid dereliction
  I saw a form, a splendour past comparing,
And felt, in rotting damp and cold constriction,
  As if death spilled a spring of life whose potion   20
  Gave warmth and made me free in that affliction.
That form, what mystery of thrilled emotion!
  Divine conception traced here, still enduring!
  One look that bore me to that flooding ocean
From which augmented higher forms come pouring.   25
  Mysterious vessel, oracles declaring!
  Let fittingly me breach your dank immuring;
In humble hand you, treasured prize, now bearing
  To open air, to sense in contemplation,
  I turn with reverence to the sunlight flaring.   30
Has life for man a higher aspiration
  Than God-in-Nature open to his seeing?:
  Who turns to spirit matter's liquidation,
  Who keeps the spirit's work in constant being.

Dornburg, September 1828

Früh, wenn Tal, Gebirg und Garten
Nebelschleiern sich enthüllen,
Und dem sehnlichsten Erwarten
Blumenkelche bunt sich füllen,

Wenn der Äther, Wolken tragend,   5
Mit dem klaren Tage streitet,
Und ein Ostwind, sie verjagend,
Blaue Sonnenbahn bereitet,

Dankst du dann, am Blick dich weidend,
Reiner Brust der Großen, Holden,   10
Wird die Sonne, rötlich scheidend,
Rings den Horizont vergolden.

Dem Aufgehenden Vollmonde

Dornburg, 25 August 1828

Willst du mich sogleich verlassen?
Warst im Augenblick so nah!
Dich umfinstern Wolkenmassen,
Und nun bist du gar nicht da.

Doch du fühlst, wie ich betrübt bin,   5
Blickt dein Rand herauf als Stern!
Zeugest mir, daß ich geliebt bin,
Sei das Liebchen noch so fern.

So hinan denn! hell und heller,
Reiner Bahn, in voller Pracht!   10
Schlägt mein Herz auch schmerzlich schneller,
Überselig ist die Nacht.

Ein Gleichnis

Jüngst pflückt ich einen Wiesenstrauß,
Trug ihn gedankenvoll nach Haus,
Da hatten von der warmen Hand
Die Kronen sich alle zur Erde gewandt.
Ich setzte sie in frisches Glas,   5
Und welch ein Wunder war mir das!

Dornburg, September 1828 (1828)

When, in garden, valley, mountains,
Dawn through misty veils is spilling,
Colours fill the flowers as fountains,
Every utmost longing stilling,

When the ether clouding over   5
Clarity of day oppresses
And the East Wind, airy drover,
Clears the blue as sun progresses,

If you feast your eyes then, purely,
Thank the gracious great one truly,   10
Parting sun shall redden surely,
Gild the whole horizon newly.

To the Full Moon Rising (1828)

Dornburg, 25 August 1828

Will you leave me, how secure you?
When just now you were so near!
Clouds amassed in dark obscure you
And now you're no longer here.

But you sense how I am troubled,   5
And your rim returns as star!
That I'm loved you pledge redoubled
Even though my love be far.

Upwards on then! brighter brighten,
Coursing clear in glorious light!   10
Though my heart race, pain to heighten,
Overblissful is the night.

An Equation (1828)

Some flowers from the fields I sought
And took them home with many a thought;
But then from my warm hand I found
The crowns all drooping to the ground.
I put them in a fresh-filled glass   5
And what a marvel came to pass!

Die Köpfchen hoben sich empor,
Die Blätterstengel im grünen Flor,
Und allzusammen so gesund
Als stünden sie noch auf Muttergrund.　　10

So war mir's als ich wundersam
Mein Lied in fremder Sprache vernahm.

Vermächtnis

Kein Wesen kann zu Nichts zerfallen!
Das Ew'ge regt sich fort in allen,
Am Sein erhalte dich beglückt!
Das Sein ist ewig; denn Gesetze
Bewahren die lebend'gen Schätze,　　5
Aus welchen sich das All geschmückt.

Das Wahre war schon längst gefunden,
Hat edle Geisterschaft verbunden,
Das alte Wahre, faß es an!
Verdank es, Erdensohn, dem Weisen,　　10
Der ihr die Sonne zu umkreisen
Und dem Geschwister wies die Bahn.

Sofort nun wende dich nach innen,
Das Zentrum findest du da drinnen,
Woran kein Edler zweifeln mag.　　15
Wirst keine Regel da vermissen,
Denn das selbständige Gewissen
Ist Sonne deinem Sittentag.

Den Sinnen hast du dann zu trauen,
Kein Falsches lassen sie dich schauen,　　20
Wenn dein Verstand dich wach erhält.
Mit frischem Blick bemerke freudig,
Und wandle sicher wie geschmeidig
Durch Auen reichbegabter Welt.

Genieße mäßig Füll' und Segen,　　25
Vernunft sei überall zugegen,
Wo Leben sich des Lebens freut.
Dann ist Vergangenheit beständig,
Das Künftige voraus lebendig,
Der Augenblick ist Ewigkeit.　　30

The heads were standing up once more,
The leaves and stalks green as before,
All flourishing as with new birth,
As if they still stood in their mother earth.   10

Just so I felt when I heard my song sung
Marvellously strange in an alien tongue.

Testament (1829)

No being can be annihilated!
In all things life's perpetuated,
Hold on to being and feel blessed!
It is eternal; lawful measure
Preserves the ever-living treasure   5
In which the universe is dressed.

The true is found and known for ever
And joins all noble minds together,
The ancient truth perceive and hold!
To the sage give thanks now, earthling,   10
Who ordered round the sun earth's circling
And orbits to the planets told.

At once in to yourself now enter
And there within you find the centre
Undoubted by the noble mind.   15
In there you'll find all regulated:
In conscience free and activated
The sun of moral life you find.

Then trust your senses for your vision,
Preventing falsity's misprision   20
By commonsense kept on the mark.
With insight fresh observing blithely
Then wander certainly and lithely
About this world's endowered park.

Let moderation's joys sustain you   25
And reason's presence entertain you
Where life is life's felicity.
The past's forever re-created,
The future here anticipated,
The moment is eternity.   30

Und war es endlich dir gelungen,
Und bist du vom Gefühl durchdrungen:
Was fruchtbar ist, allein ist wahr,
Du prüfst das allgemeine Walten,
Es wird nach seiner Weise schalten,   35
Geselle dich zur kleinsten Schar.

Und wie von alters her im stillen
Ein Liebewerk nach eignem Willen
Der Philosoph, der Dichter schuf,
So wirst du schönste Gunst erzielen: 40
Denn edlen Seelen vorzufühlen
Ist wünschenswertester Beruf.

Chinesisch-deutsch Jahres- und Tageszeiten

I

Sag', was könnt' uns Mandarinen,
Satt zu herrschen, müd zu dienen,
Sag', was könnt' uns übrigbleiben,
Als in solchen Frühlingstagen
Uns des Nordens zu entschlagen   5
Und am Wasser und im Grünen
Fröhlich trinken, geistig schreiben,
Schal' auf Schale, Zug in Zügen?

II

Weiß wie Lilien, reine Kerzen,
Sternen gleich, bescheidner Beugung,
Leuchtet aus dem Mittelherzen,
Rot gesäumt, die Glut der Neigung.

So frühzeitige Narzissen   5
Blühen reihenweis im Garten.
Mögen wohl die guten wissen,
Wen sie so spaliert erwarten.

III

Ziehn die Schafe von der Wiese,
Liegt sie da, ein reines Grün;
Aber bald zum Paradiese
Wird sie bunt geblümt erblühn.

And finally when you've achieved it
And in each fibre you perceive it:
In fruitfulness is truth's true test,
You judge society's ruling passion,
It carries on in its own fashion,   35
And find the smallest company best.

And just as to the life secluded
Philosophers and poets are mooded
And thus their work of love was cast,
You too will seek high grace and merits: 40
For to prefigure noble spirits
Is a vocation unsurpassed.

Chinese-German Hours and Seasons (1827–30)

I

Tell us mandarins enquiring,
Sated rulers, servants tiring,
Tell, what's left us except yearning
To be quit when spring's around us,
Shaking off the North that bound us,   5
And by ponds, on grass reclining,
Gaily drink, write wit and learning,
Cup on cup, brushed strokes entwining?

II

Pure as candles, lilies' whiteness,
Starlike, bowed in modest station,
From the middle heart shines brightness,
Red-hemmed glow of inclination.

Thus narcissi prematurely   5
Bloom along the garden border.
Only they can know, though, surely
Whom they wait for ranked in order.

III

From the meadow sheep are leaving,
There it lies, a purest green;
Soon though, Paradise conceiving,
It will bloom with flowering sheen.

Hoffnung breitet lichte Schleier
Nebelhaft vor unsern Blick:
Wunscherfüllung, Sonnenfeier,
Wolkenteilung bring' uns Glück!

5

IV

Der Pfau schreit häßlich, aber sein Geschrei
Erinnert mich ans himmlische Gefieder,
So ist mir auch sein Schreien nicht zuwider.
Mit indischen Gänsen ist's nicht gleicherlei,
Sie zu erdulden, ist unmöglich:
Die häßlichen, sie schreien unerträglich.

5

V

Entwickle deiner Lüste Glanz
Der Abendsonne goldnen Strahlen,
Laß deines Schweifes Rad und Kranz
Kühn-äugelnd ihr entgegen prahlen.
Sie forscht, wo es im Grünen blüht,
Im Garten, überwölbt vom Blauen;
Ein Liebespaar, wo sie's ersieht,
Glaubt sie das Herrlichste zu schauen.

5

VI

Der Guckuck wie die Nachtigall,
Sie möchten den Frühling fesseln,
Doch drängt der Sommer schon überall
Mit Disteln und mit Nesseln.
Auch mir hat er das leichte Laub
An jenem Baum verdichtet,
Durch das ich sonst zu schönstem Raub
Den Liebesblick gerichtet;
Verdeckt ist mir das bunte Dach,
Die Gitter und die Pfosten;
Wohin mein Auge spähend brach,
Dort ewig bleibt mein Osten.

5

10

VII

War schöner als der schönste Tag,
Drum muß man mir verzeihen,
Daß ich sie nicht vergessen mag,
Am wenigsten im Freien.
Im Garten war's, sie kam heran,

5

Light of hope is permeating   5
Outspread veils of misty shrouds:
Wants fulfilled, sun celebrating,
Happiness, break through the clouds!

IV

The peacock's cry is horrid, but his call
Reminds me that his plumage is celestial,
And so for me his cry is not too bestial.
But Indian Geese are not the same at all,
Listening to them is quite impossible: 5
They're horrid, and their cry is just not tolerable.

V

When evening sun's gold rays pour down
Resplendently unfurl your desires,
Revolve your bold-eyed train and crown
And match him with your boastful fires.
He seeks what's flowering in the green,   5
What's in the garden blue-sky vaulted;
And where there's lovers to be seen
He knows he sees what's most exalted.

VI

The cuckoo and the nightingale
Cast spells so spring may settle,
But summer thrusts and soon makes them fail
With the thistle and the nettle.
On my tree now the leaves' light weft   5
Is densely concentrated
Through which for love's most lovely theft
My eye once penetrated;
Now lattice, doors, and roof bright-crowned
Are covered altogether;   10
That place my searching eye once found
Remains my East forever.

VII

Than fairest day she was more fair
And so I beg your pardon
That I recall her everywhere
And more so in a garden.
It was a garden, she drew near   5

Mir ihre Gunst zu zeigen;
Das fühl' ich noch und denke dran
Und bleib' ihr ganz zu eigen.

VIII

Dämmrung senkte sich von oben,
Schon ist alle Nähe fern;
Doch zuerst emporgehoben
Holden Lichts der Abendstern!
Alles schwankt ins Ungewisse,   5
Nebel schleichen in die Höh';
Schwarzvertiefte Finsternisse
Widerspiegelnd ruht der See.

Nun im östlichen Bereiche
Ahn' ich Mondenglanz und -glut,   10
Schlanker Weiden Haargezweige
Scherzen auf der nächsten Flut.
Durch bewegter Schatten Spiele
Zittert Lunas Zauberschein,
Und durchs Auge schleicht die Kühle   15
Sänftigend ins Herz hinein.

IX

Nun weiß man erst, was Rosenknospe sei,
Jetzt, da die Rosenzeit vorbei;
Ein Spätling noch am Stocke glänzt
Und ganz allein die Blumenwelt ergänzt.

X

Als Allerschönste bist du anerkannt,
Bist Königin des Blumenreichs genannt;
Unwidersprechlich allgemeines Zeugnis,
Streitsucht verbannend, wundersam Ereignis!
Du bist es also, bist kein bloßer Schein,   5
In dir trifft Schaun und Glauben überein;
Doch Forschung strebt und ringt, ermüdend nie,
Nach dem Gesetz, dem Grund Warum und Wie.

XI

'Mich ängstigt das Verfängliche
Im widrigen Geschwätz,
Wo nichts verharret, alles flieht,
Wo schon verschwunden, was man sieht;

And so her favour rendered;
I feel it still and mind it dear
And stay to her surrendered.

VIII

Twilight down from high has drifted,
What was near's already far;
First, though, high above is lifted
Graced in light the evening star!
All on imprecision verges, 5
To the heights the mists slow snake;
Darkness into blackness merges
Mirrored in the resting lake.

Now I sense the moonlight presses
Ardent in the evening sky; 10
Slender willows' branching tresses
Jest upon the wave nearby.
Luna's quivering spell is glowing
Where the shadows play and dart,
Coolness through the eye is flowing 15
Soothingly into the heart.

IX

Only now do we know the rosebud at last,
Now when the time for roses has passed;
On the stem a laggard's shining still,
Singly the world of flowers to fulfil.

X

Most beautiful of all you are acclaimed,
In the realm of flowers as queen you are named;
Unanswerable general testament,
Banishing conflict, marvellous event!
You truly are, not merely so appear, 5
In you belief agrees with vision clear;
Yet science strives and struggles, never tires,
For law and cause, for Why and How enquires.

XI

'Theorising's reprehensible,
I fear its snares and fret
Where nothing stays and all things flee,
Where disappears the thing we see;

Und mich umfängt das bängliche,   5
Das graugestrickte Netz.' –
Getrost! Das Unvergängliche,
Es ist das ewige Gesetz,
Wonach die Ros' und Lilie blüht.

XII
'Hingesunken alten Träumen,
Buhlst mit Rosen, sprichst mit Bäumen
Statt der Mädchen, statt der Weisen;
Können das nicht löblich preisen,   5
Kommen deshalb die Gesellen,
Sich zur Seite dir zu stellen,
Finden, dir und uns zu dienen,
Pinsel, Farbe, Wein im Grünen.'

XIII
Die stille Freude wollt ihr stören?
Laßt mich bei meinem Becher Wein;
Mit andern kann man sich belehren,
Begeistert wird man nur allein.

XIV
'Nun denn! Eh' wir von hinnen eilen,
Hast noch was Kluges mitzuteilen?'

Sehnsucht ins Ferne, Künftige zu beschwichtigen,
Beschäftige dich hier und heut im Tüchtigen.

*

Es spricht sich aus der stumme Schmerz,
Der Äther klärt sich blau und bläuer,
Da schwebt sie ja, die goldne Leier,
Komm, alte Freundin, komm ans Herz.

Grey fears incomprehensible 5
Enmesh me in their net.' –
Fear not! The indestructible
In the eternal law is set
By which the rose and lily be.

XII

'Man's old dreaming here disposes,
Trees you talk to, fondle roses,
Girls and sages you're excluding;
That won't do, for ever brooding,
That's why now together banding 5
By your side your friends are standing,
Help for you and us, we're thinking,
Is colour, brush, on green lawns drinking.'

XIII

Why now disturb my quiet elation?
Leave me with my wine alone.
With others one gets education
But inspiration on one's own.

XIV

'Well now! Before we dash away
Haven't you something wise to say?'
Pining for Far and Future is assuaged
If here and now you're solidly engaged.

*

The speechless pain has said its part,
Clearer blue and bluer clears the air,
The golden lyre, look, hovering there,
Come, my old friend, come to my heart.

NOTES

---

[1] A dramatic satire on the itinerant soap-box preachers of the time promoting their own personal sects, and also on the over-simplistic followers of Rousseau's call for a return to nature. See also Introduction, p. xvii.

[2] Amadis is a hero of fifteenth- and sixteenth-century Iberian romance. Prince Pipi and Princess Fish probably derive from French fairy tales.

[3] In Goethe's play on the Dutch struggle for independence from Spain, *Egmont* (published 1787), this song is sung by the hero's beloved Klärchen, a young bourgeois woman who, after Egmont is imprisoned and sentenced to death by the Spanish, commits suicide.

[4] Johannes Secundus was a sixteenth-century Dutch poet who wrote in Latin, author of a series of passionate sensual poems called *Basia* ('kisses'). Goethe retained a kindred feeling for him throughout his life.

[5] The reference is not to the political triumvirates of Pompey, Crassus, and Caesar or to Mark Antony, Lepidus, and Octavian, but to the Latin love poets Catullus, Propertius, and Tibullus, who were inspired in the same way as the poet of these elegies.

[6] In the story told by Rabelais and Lafontaine, Hans Carvel dreamt that he was given a ring which, so long as he wore it, would ensure his wife's fidelity. He woke to find around his finger a ring of a different kind.

[7] The poem addresses the enthusiastic proponents of the Romantic idealist philosophy of F. W. J. Schelling (1775–1854).

[8] The allusion is to Wilhelm von Schütz's play *Lacrimas* (1803), which uses an array of Romantic verse forms.

[9] The riddle in this poem on the words *Herz* ('heart'), *lieb* ('dear', 'beloved'), and *herzlieb* ('dearest' or 'darling') cannot be reproduced in English. The sonnet came about as a result of a competition between Goethe, the Romantic playwright Zacharias Werner, and the classicist F. W. Riemer to compose a sonnet in honour

of Wilhelmine Herzlieb, the eighteen-year-old ward of the Jena bookseller Frommann.

[10]Tibullus, *Elegies*, I.v.39–40.

[11]'iste' is the Latin pronoun 'this (one)' or 'that (one)'. Later in the poem it is called 'Meister Iste', translated here as 'Master' in the sense of the craft-guilds as one who has skill and authority. A literal translation 'Master That One' can also carry in English the connotation of an unruly boy.

[12]In Greek drama the *epirrhema* is a verse that follows a chorus and in which the chorus leader addresses the audience. An *antepirrhema* is a second such verse.

[13]Nepomuk, a fourteenth-century Vicar General of Prague, was drowned in the Moldau on the orders of Wenceslas IV because he opposed royal interference in clerical prerogatives and, according to legend, because he refused to betray to the King the Queen's confidences given to him under the seal of the confessional.

[14]Some years after this poem was written some public misunderstanding of its implications prompted Goethe to respond with 'Testament' (p. 151).

SELECT BIBLIOGRAPHY

Publications of the English Goethe Society (PEGS), vols i–xii (1886–1912) and New Series vols i- (1924–) published by W. S. Maney, contain a range of articles in English on all aspects of Goethe's life and work. See A. C. Weaver, *Index to the P.E.G.S. 1886–1970* (Leeds, 1973).

Selected English translations of Goethe's works:

Goethe's Collected Works, various translators, 12 vols (New York, 1983–9; Princeton, 1994–5)
Elective Affinities, tr. David Constantine (Oxford, 1994)
Faust, Part One, tr. David Luke (Oxford, 1987)
Faust, Part Two, tr. David Luke (Oxford, 1994)
Goethe's Poems of the West and the East: West-Eastern Divan (West-Östlicher Divan), tr. John Whaley (Berne, 1998)
The Sorrows of Young Werther, tr. Michael Hulse (Harmondsworth, 1989)
Torquato Tasso, tr. Alan Brownjohn (London, 1985)

Biography:

Nicholas Boyle, *Goethe: The Poet and the Age, vol. 1: The Poetry of Desire* (Oxford, 1991)
Richard Friedenthal, *Goethe. His Life and Times* (London, 1965)
G. H. Lewes, *The Life and Works of Goethe* (London, 1855, reprinted 1949)

Cultural and intellectual context:

W. H. Bruford, *Germany in the Eighteenth Century: The Social Background of the Literary Revival* (Cambridge, 1952)
——, *Culture and Society in Classical Weimar, 1775–1806* (Cambridge, 1962)
Alan Menhennet, *Order and Freedom: Literature and Society in Germany, 1720–1805* (London, 1973)
Roy Pascal, *The German Sturm und Drang* (Manchester, 1953)

Literary criticism:

M. H. Abrams, *Natural Supernaturalism: Tradition and Revolution in Romantic Literature* (New York, 1971)

Eric A. Blackall, *Goethe and the Novel* (Ithaca, NY, 1976)

S. Burkhardt, *The Drama of Language* (Baltimore and London, 1970)

Barker Fairley, *A Study of Goethe* (Oxford, 1947)

——, *Faust: Six Essays* (Oxford, 1953)

F. J. Lamport, *German Classical Drama* (Cambridge, 1989)

T. J. Reed, *The Classical Centre: Goethe and Weimar, 1775–1832* (London, 1980)

Hans Reiss, *Goethe's Novels* (London, 1969)

Martin Swales, *Goethe: The Sorrows of Young Werther* (Cambridge, 1987)

Humphrey Trevelyan, *Goethe and the Greeks* (Cambridge, 1941, reprinted 1981)

E. M. Wilkinson, T. J. Reed et al., *Goethe Revisited* (London, 1984)

E. M. Wilkinson and L. A. Willoughby, *Goethe: Poet and Thinker* (London, 1962)

John R. Williams, *Goethe's Faust* (London, 1987)

Scientific ideas:

Matthew Bell, *Goethe's Naturalistic Anthropology: Man and Other Plants* (Oxford, 1994)

H. B. Nisbet, *Goethe and the Scientific Tradition* (London, 1972)

G. A. Wells, *Goethe and the Development of Science, 1750–1900* (Alphen, 1978)

INDEX OF ENGLISH TITLES

INDEX OF ENGLISH FIRST LINES

INDEX OF GERMAN TITLES

INDEX OF GERMAN FIRST LINES